Perfectionism

Overcome Perfectionism in the Pursuit of Success

(A Step-by-step Approach to Overcoming Perfectionism and Procrastination)

Roger Nelson

Published By **Regina Loviusher**

Roger Nelson

Perfectionism: Overcome Perfectionism in the Pursuit of Success (A Step-by-step Approach to Overcoming Perfectionism and Procrastination)

ISBN   978-1-77485-685-7

Legal & Disclaimer

information provided by this guide. This disclaimer applies to any damages or injury caused by the use and application, whether directly or indirectly, of any advice or information presented, whether for breach of contract, tort, negligence, personal injury, criminal intent, or under any other cause of action.

You agree to accept all risks of using the information presented inside this book. You need to consult a professional medical practitioner in order to ensure you are both able and healthy enough to participate in this program.

TABLE OF CONTENTS

Introduction

Teens are often viewed as naturally temperamental, moody, and rebellious. They desire independence but must learn become responsible and maintain the independence they desire. Many find that the teenage time is a tense period. There are numerous choices that teens must make on their own. There is constant pressure to act and act in a certain manner and they're just getting to know about who they are and what they would like to be. The pressure they experience from their peers is felt in their minds and may even depress their thoughts.

Unfortunately, adolescents aren't explicitly taught how to manage emotions or react properly in social situations. While they might be taught how to behave but there is usually no option for the best way to respond. Teenagers must make many difficult choices throughout their adolescent days. While some can breeze through this phase, others are left to suffer in silence.

The amount of teens who cover up their depression, anxiety and fear of being judged is overwhelming. These are the years that are supposed to be the most fulfilling of their lives. Many find them an ongoing battle.

How they view themselves in these years will determine what they will think about themselves when they become adults. The way they deal with their thoughts, emotions, and their behavior during these years can make or break their progress. What many teenagers are lacking is their ability to recognize and connect their thoughts, emotions and actions?

While they concentrate on schoolwork or making friends and playing football but they don't think about examining their beliefs or feelings. They can be constantly fighting an unflattering self-image, restrictive beliefs, or intense fears simply because they don't want deal with them or aren't sure how to. In addition, teens today are obsessed with social media, and it's leading them to be very ineffective. The technological age is huge and is taking them by storm.

Cognitive Behavioral Therapy is a way to provide teens with the understanding and tools needed to release the things that are hindering them from reaching their goals. The therapy deals with the behaviors, thoughts and emotions that lead a teenager to behave in a way that is out of their control. They may also become isolated from his or her friends, and get back in class. Once you are enrolled in Cognitive Behavioral Therapy, you learn to recognize your negative thoughts and the power they hold and the ways to take control of them.

Cognitive Behavioral Therapy (CBT) is based on an established scientific basis. The book won't overpower you with a wealth of data from the empirical however, it will present the evidence to show that CBT is scientifically proven and is beyond a mere concept of positivity.

Within the United States alone, more than 40 million suffer each day with one or several types of anxiety disorders. Phobias, major depressions and social anxiety are one of many examples, but there are a myriad of them and a variety of disorders fall into this category.

One of these conditions one of these is called Post-Traumatic stress Disorder (PTSD). When soldiers return from war, they are unable to adjust to the calm of a more civilian setting. The most frequent association with PTSD is with soldiers but it is not true to think that they are the sole population affected by it. Post-Traumatic Stress Disorder is experienced by a broad range of people around the world. Teachers, businessmen and taxi drivers...no one is exempt from suffering.

What can you expect to see:

Learn to recognize what is essential to your life, what beliefs and opinions you hold about yourself, and also how to conquer anxiety and thoughts that are negative.

Each section covers a distinct area that will, at the end, help you to establish clear goals and make the necessary changes which will not just impact your teenage years but affect your adult life. While you are reading the content, be careful not to jumping ahead. Read each section and respond to the questions that pop up.

It's helpful to keep an organized journal to traverse each step. It will provide you with an opportunity to ask questions and , more importantly, allow you to record your progression. Journals provide you with an outline of the guide can be used to recall what you want to achieve in your life.

For Teens

The information on these pages can help you in different ways. Be willing and open to complete the exercises and track the questions you are asked. The course will help you understand the reasons behind your struggle in various aspects of your life. It will help you believe that you are able to overcome any challenge that you may face.

For Parents

Although this book is targeted to help teens overcome difficulties they face but don't overlook how the information contained found in this book can help you too. With your teen, finish the exercise and learn the strategies. The majority of the materials include additional information that is specifically targeted for you. There are tips and tricks that will assist your child to adopt new ideas and behavior. You'll also discover ways to recognize the signs that your child is struggling, and strategies for dealing with large emotions and difficult situations.

This book will not just inspire your teenager to learn the abilities that will help them in the future, but will help them grow to become confident, successful women and men.

Procrastination Causes and Effects

Procrastination is , and is always been the stealer of time. Everybody has been a prey to the habit of procrastination at one moment in our lives. This happens to us in all the things we do. Instead of taking action immediately we often put it off until later. the task until later. This can lead to emotional burdens as we are left to regret having spent time. This usually happens when we come to the realization that there's no ideal moment to do something that we originally put off.

The most painful aspect of procrastination is that they affect our productivity in a variety of ways. In the first place, you'll never accomplish anything because you will always have an excuse for you to finish an activity in a later time or at a later time. If you begin to develop a pattern of putting off work, it will go into affecting both your physical and mental overall well-being. Your self-esteem can be negatively affected because you don't feel confident in what you are doing. You make a promise to yourself that you will get up early in the morning to finish your assignment, and you get up 4 hours behind on your timetable.

It's quite frustrating. The worst part is that you are caught in a loop that you aren't able to finish your tasks in time. There is no motive to be blamed for what's occurring to you. However, the good thing is that there's an option to fix this. Many people face the same issue as you. Therefore, don't worry that you're experiencing your own issues.

Chapter 1: The Social Media/Phone

Addiction And Time Wasted On Both
How Do Phones Affect Our Attention Time

Moreover, social media addiction ends up creating digital zombies. The millennial generation cannot form genuine human connections due to their obsession with their phones.

For instance, two students waiting in a room to wait for an event to begin. In the modern world it is commonplace for them to spend their free time on their smartphones and then go directly to their meeting. While in the meeting they'll likely leave their mobiles on the desk and continuously attempt to peek at their notifications, awaiting for the next dose of dopamine to fulfill the impulses triggered by FOMO.

Let's take a look at similar scenarios if phones were removed from the equation.

The two students sitting in the waiting room would have the opportunity to engage with each other. It could allow them to start a conversation about this issue and allow the formation of an eventual relationship and friendship.

However when they are not using their phones at their desks during meetings and the two students can be more engaged in the discussion that is taking place within the group, and be more attentive to their surroundings and engage with the discussions and issues in the room.

With no distractions of who's messaging them or how many new friends they have on their smartphones Their focus will be on solving issues and come up with innovative ideas. A lack of smartphones within the room will dramatically increase the focus of employees and have a positive impact on the efficiency of the company. Additionally, when there's greater awareness within the room and issues are addressed faster, students can concentrate on implementing the solutions.

Another instance of how much addiction to phone use affects addiction is in interpersonal relationships.

It's not unusual to see families browsing their phones at dinner. In the past, dinner is a time to share how everyone's day went and chat with the other following a working day that was hectic.

It is now common that people don't bother talking to one another or engaging in conversations. They prefer to eat and scroll on their mobiles. It is now the standard notion of unwinding after a tiring day.

The impact of this behaviour is evident in many teens as they enter adulthood. They can find it difficult to focus on the world that is happening around them. The millennials and Gen Z tend to view things through the filter of social media and their dependence on digital media alters their perspective on the world.

As an example, suppose you're in the middle of a holiday along with the family. You see a stunning sunset at the beach, and the first thought that pops up in your mind is "Wow these colors are incredible, I'll take an image of it and share it online". Then you'll be spending the next half hour striving to get every hue of hue until the sky turns dark.

Then you could spend an hour looking for the ideal image among these pictures, and when you are content with a few photos, you begin editing them, enhancing the pictures to make them appear more impressive than they actually are.

Once you've finished improving the image, you can try to think of an intriguing caption. It's likely that you've spent so many hours creating this post that you're not aware of the wonderful time you had relaxing on a tranquil beach, enjoying the gorgeous sunset with your loved ones.

A decade later you'll not recall the time you spent taking an image to post on the internet and you wouldn't even care the number of likes you've received for an Instagram post.

However, what you'd have remembered are the stories you'd have told relatives. The look on your mother's face or your brother's wacky smile. These are the moments the generation we live in is being left out of and we aren't even aware of it.

Our focus is diverted away from the things that are important to what is important. We aren't thinking about the long-term as we're too focused on quick-term gains.

A lot of our time is absorbed and diverted. Every minute spent to our mobiles is a loss of time, precious memories and even creativity. Our attention spans are decreasing. It's difficult to focus on just one thing at a time.

Even when we're spending time with our loved ones and friends, we are constantly going through our phones. While working or studying We constantly check our messages. As time passes, the wiring of our brains alters and we lose sight of our own thoughts.

Inattention to detail can hinder our work. We can get less accomplished, even though we have more time. We're incapable of remembering things because we were not paying attention . Our brain gets less efficient as time passes.

How can we address this issue?

Digital Addiction doesn't have to become the final word for us. We've seen that digital minimalism can be a solution to some of the problems due to our dependence on our smartphones. The only thing we have to become aware of what effects it can have on our lives. If we can identify an issue, it is easy to address.

In order to ensure that our smartphone does not always take up too many of our attention the first thing you should do is to turn off notifications. Many apps have an inbuilt feature that lets users to disable notifications for a set period or even mute them completely.

If you don't have urgent messages to check, it is recommended to switch off notifications for text messages, particularly during meetings or with your family members.

Furthermore, if it makes you feel depressed every time you glance at social media, and find yourself feeling pressured to keep updating and checking for likes. Also that, if social media take all part of your day, then you're better to not use the services for any reason.

You can opt to get rid completely from the app or disable notifications for the application and its features such as comments and likes. Even if you only post occasionally your phone will not inform you when someone has left an appreciation or comments on your photo and you won't have to keep looking to see the number of people who saw your post or expressed thank you.

In reducing the amount of notifications that are not important and allowing you to pay attention to important notifications. There will be no need to pick your phone repeatedly again. It will be free of the anxiety and anxiety that comes from waiting for a message or anticipating people to like you. You'll experience greater focus and be able to focus on other activities which are more satisfying and crucial.

If you're not feeling the need to keep checking your phone, it's possible to converse with those in front of you. Instead of checking notifications in meetings, you are able to contribute to the conversation that is going on. You can propose ideas and solutions and be perceived as being present in the present.

The millennial generation is always looking for opportunities and jobs that will make them feel as if they're creating a positive impact or making a difference. If you're more engaged in your conversations, you'll naturally find that your thoughts are taken into consideration, and you'll be better able to think critically in your work and on projects. This way, your course becomes clearer since your mind isn't occupied by distracting thoughts. You'll notice an improvement in your mental performance generally.

If you happen to be at the top of a mountain, will be able to enjoy the stunning scenery around you, as well as the blue skies that are above you. The first thought you'll have will not be "let me take a snap photograph." You won't spend time trying to get the perfect photo and you won't get stuck on your phone trying edit it.

In actual fact when you've gotten rid of images of Facebook and the likes out of your thoughts and you are able to fully be able to appreciate the beauty around you. It is possible to breathe into the fresh scent of air, take in the sights at beautiful nature, and your mind will be able to enjoy an inner peace.

These moments could provide you a new perspective on your life. These are the exact moments you're wasting by spending all of your time and time worrying about notifications or focusing on social media.

Time: Online when it makes sense

Let's face it, the fact that the addiction to smartphones is a major source of our time won't be a shock to anyone. A lot of us don't think about the amount of time we've spent using our mobiles. Even if we do not stare at the phone for an extended duration, we'll check your phone in order to read our messages or get notifications.

It's difficult to determine the amount of time we're using our smartphones. However, if we look back and consider the number of minutes, seconds and hours are spent on social media and our smartphones, we might be astonished by the results.

The average adult spends about 2 hours a day on their mobile phones. This may appear to be a huge number, but bear in mind that, assuming we are up all day, two hours of using our phones each day is 16 percent of the time we're awake using our phones. This is because of other addictive aspects of social media and apps.

It is possible to check your phone and check your messages. The friend you are with could send you an image or video. So you can go to another application. After you've liked the video, you browse the site to view additional videos. You then share a few of them with your acquaintances and spend quite a lot of time using your phone.

In the same way it is if, after an exhausting morning at work, you're browsing Instagram looking through pictures and zooming through "story" reels. When you look at a specific article, you may notice a link to a separate section or page. This could lead you to a different section of Instagram.

Perhaps you've wanted to sit down to an enjoyable film after getting home, or perhaps you wanted to contact an old acquaintance you've not seen in a long time. Perhaps you have a lot of work that you need to attend to or deadlines fast coming up.

It's time to say goodbye to all that since that quick glance at Instagram will cost you an whole hour. It's a constant scrolling and glancing at numerous websites and devouring an inordinate amount of content that you've lost the track of the time. Then you're exhausted and unable to concentrate You realize that it's late to be doing anything else, and you decide to switch off your mobile and get to bed.

Similar to that, we may be spending time with our phones in the classroom, during recess and lunch break, or or during our commute. In every phase that we go through, we're being wasting time on the internet and our mobiles. The clock is never waiting for anyone and time is priced higher than any other.

Imagine if one is spending 15% of the brief day on their phone How much time will an individual who is dependent or obsessed with their smartphones spend.

If you're a lot dependent on your smartphone, you could be spending 30-40% of the time on social media, messaging playing games, or checking for notifications. The time could easily be used for something more productive.

Many of us are sad because we do not have enough time to pursue our goals. There are always other projects that we would like to tackle, or we may want to try something new or enjoy more time spending with our friends and family. If we're spending our time using our smartphones it is a chance removed from us.

As you observe these goals and expectations disappear from your reach that causes us to feel unhappy over our lives. It also make us feel as if we don't have enough time to do things or do the things we truly would like to do.

But, in actuality, the time is available to us or would be should we be able to stop ourselves from spending days with our smartphones.

The notion that no change is possible to bring about in a hurry has been proven throughout the book. It is important to keep in mind that to achieve anything, you must be patient.

The first step in getting to your goal is understanding what you really would like to achieve. The most common reason that people get off course when they are trying to achieve a goal is that they are not clear enough about what they really would like to achieve.

The idea of saying, "I'll just spend less time on my phone" does not give you the goal you want to achieve. Instead telling yourself "I will be spending just 40 minutes each day" this gives you a clearer view. The objective becomes quantifiable.

Find out how much time you're spending using your mobile regularly. It shouldn't be a problem considering the number of apps on the market that are aimed at helping you complete the challenge of minimising your digital usage. The apps collect the data from your daily use and provide you a clear graph or chart, so that you are able to easily figure out how much time you have to reduce. The results might be alarming initially, but you've discovered the issue and can solve it efficiently.

Sometimes, self-determination isn't enough. You might need extra help. Although it might sound odd, you can make use of applications to block apps and keep users from using their phone repeatedly. There are numerous apps that lock or timers can stop users from using the app for a specified amount of time. You can turn off the timers when you need to complete a task that is important or during times when you typically spend time on your smartphone.

There are some people who's messages must be responded to regardless of what. If you're not on your mobile for a long period of time, it could be a source of concern to your family and acquaintances that you've been away for that long. If you pull out your phone to answer those messages you receive, you could get distracted and spending a lot more time using the phone that you have to. In no time you'll be back to where you started to sink into the same pit of addiction to phones.

Do not fret though. There's a simple technology solution too. There are apps that let you send texts automatically. Perhaps you can use some of them to text an email that reads "Hey! I'm off for a couple of hours. I'll be back around 10.30 p.m." (or some other information that informs anyone who is trying to find you how to contact you.

Another option is to leave an open post or send an email stating that you'll not be on your cell phone for a few days and provide alternative ways to reach you, or an approximate time you'll be in contact.

This step may seem a bit excessive for some, but if something else that to work for you, then the best option to stop your obsession and reduce time is to uninstall your social media accounts such as Facebook, Instagram, and Snapchat as well as any games or other apps you may utilize longer than you need to.

There's a saying that goes, "Outta sight outta mind." This method is quite similar to the one above. If you don't have the apps installed on your phone, you will not always be able to find notifications or attempt to access these apps as you'll be aware that there is no reason to. Each every time you unlock your phone you'll be reminded that it's not worth using your phone because the apps you use frequently aren't there anymore.

If you are absolutely required to use social media, let yourself check your feeds at least once every day for a short amount of time on your laptop. This way, you don't have to use any phone.

What do you accomplish with all the extra time?

After you've reduced the amount of time you use your phone, you'll discover how much time you actually have.

The weekends no longer feel like they're a bit short, and you'll be able to have more time to spend on weekdays. You'll see that, even though you're always on the go but there are long times within your routine that are available to do other activities.

There will also be tiny periods of time that are free like when you're taking the elevator or getting an Uber ride, or waiting in line for your cookies to finish cooking in the oven. These short periods are a great opportunity to let yourself unwind and take a breather.

Your mind will be at ease and you can take a few moments to breathe deeply and enjoy the simple act of not doing anything. You'll feel more refreshed when you've had a moment to yourself, and will be more focused on whatever task you are working on.

In the future, you'll also have endless hours of leisure. As has been mentioned that many of us have other projects we wish to complete or are too busy to have time for family and friends.

There is plenty of time available. You can make use of an extended period of time to do whatever you want to do.

Chapter 2: How To Act And Shift Your

Mind-Set About Things Differently

If you are faced with a dilemma do you think that you will find solutions or do you believe that the problem is too difficult? The way we think lets us see opportunities once they are presented. The way we think can create an attitude of failure that blocks us from progress and makes us anxious, and hinders our ability succeed all through our life. In time, as our minds develop it is our attitude that determines who we develop into. Your mental state can define the person you are. It is possible to let your mental state be a burden on you, or your mental state could be the determining to the changes that you have to make to achieve your goals.

What is Mindset?

Mindset is how you see yourself and believe in your abilities such as your physical abilities, your intelligence and abilities. It influences how we face problems that we face in life. The mindset of a person allows them to remain resilient and stay focused to achieve their goals regardless of any challenges or challenges they might confront along the road.

For teens the importance of developing a healthy mental attitude can impact your grades, relationships as well as all other areas within your daily life. A positive mindset can help you identify and pursue what you're enthusiastic about. In addition, the attitude that you acquire during your teens will allow you to be successful in the future after high school.

Being a positive attitude and attitude in life

A positive mental attitude can result in an existence that will allow you to achieve. If you are faced with a challenge do you think of the issue as an opportunity to improve and grow and grow, or do you believe it's impossible and you'll be judged and criticized when you fail to tackle the issue in a timely manner? The first way of thinking lets you face challenges with confidence. It allows you to explore new possibilities as well as set goals and get out of your familiar zone. When we're not able to confront our problems with an attitude of confidence, we tend to assume that a lack of skills and knowledge is the reason we are unable to resolve or even overcome difficulties.

Fixed Mindset in contrast to. Growth Mindset

There are a variety of categories that your mind could fall into. The two most prevalent are fixed or the growth mentality. Kids naturally tend to be a growth-oriented person, but as they get older and confront new challenges, this mentality can shift into a fixed mindset. Understanding the various components of each of them and how they affect every aspect of your life will help you to determine what you require to do to alter your thinking to help you improve and achieve your goals that you have established for yourself.

Fixed Mindset

A fixed-minded mindset can put us in a defensive state. People who have a fixed mind tend to focus on their shortcomings. They don't have the capacity to accept constructive criticism, and thus they are not able to achieve the growth they can make to develop their skills and their lives. People with a fixed mentality tend to follow a monochrome pattern. They're either intelligent or smart or not, they can be accepted or not or they're either a success or failure.

A fixed mentality results in a need to constantly look for approval. Children are influenced by this belief as they're constantly being praised for appearing smart, instead of being acknowledged for their enthusiasm to learn. When they reach the age of teens, they focus on the notion that they are assessed by their intelligence in the event that they do not appear or conform to the standards set by their parents or their teachers. They fear becoming dissatisfied if they don't achieve the standards.

They don't pay attention to the effort that goes into achieving something, they concentrate on the final outcome. If you have a fixed mind, you tend to have thoughts which focus on:

* Not being able enhance their intelligence.

* The idea that individuals have a certain amount of intelligence that can't be altered.

* The belief that there's nothing you can do to enhance your abilities or alter your personality.

* Believing that the skills you possess are the only ones you're capable of. There is no way to develop new talents or abilities even if presented with the chance to master these skills.

Mindset of Growth Mindset

A mindset of growth is one that drives you to learn, improve and push yourself to do better at what you wish to be able to achieve. People with a growth mind-set love to explore new things, embrace the challenges and have an insatiable desire to learn more. People with a growth mindset aren't scared to experiment with new ideas because they don't fear to fail. Failure for those with a positive mind-set can be a chance to gain knowledge. Opportunities can arise from these mistakes, and a growing mindset can help individuals find these opportunities.

Every moment is an opportunity to learn with an unchanging mindset. Kids who have the opportunity to investigate their surroundings, face difficult situations, and learn from their experiences are more likely to grow into a mindset of growth. As they grow older, they can enjoy studying. They are able to feel a sense satisfaction for having put in the effort, and are not only focused on the final outcome. They recognize that things might not go the way they planned but they're competent to assess the results they achieve, and consequently, they are able to take their lessons from mistakes and implement the necessary adjustments.

Be aware that growing mindsets do not mean that you believe that they will be able to achieve anything you desire simply by affirming it. Instead, you recognize that you have to work hard to learn the necessary skills and become educated so that you can reach the goals you have set. You know that if you are determined to succeed you must practice and continually seek out ways to enhance your skills.

A person with a growth perspective will have thoughts that may include:

* Being aware that they have the ability to alter their identity.

* Being aware that they are able to improve their knowledge and increase their intelligence.

There are many ways you can enhance your skills and acquire new abilities.

The development of a mindset capable of leading you to your goals

A growth mindset can help people to establish goals, and reach the goals. When you have a mindset of growth it is clear that you have the ability to achieve your maximum potential. The potential is unlimitable. There isn't a ceiling which limits the distance you are able to take your journey. When you are a person who is growing you realize that learning and expanding your knowledge of the subjects that are important to you will require some effort, but it is well worth the time and effort.

Setting goals is an essential step in encouraging a growing mentality. However, the focus shouldn't solely be on the final outcome. Concentrating on the process and celebrating the wins during the journey is what is most important. Instead of being focused on getting an A grade in a class, concentrate on the information that you're getting instead of focusing on how this information can help your education beyond the classroom and concentrate on the effort you're putting into. The end result might take a different path than what you hoped to achieve, but it's the process you follow to reach your goals which are most important. Doing your best and being satisfied with your work is more important than anything else.

Consider your mental state as with its own voice. Your attitude will influence your communication with yourself. The more positive your attitude is, the more positively you are able to speak to yourself internally. There are a lot of things that you could be telling yourself that are limiting the things you're actually capable of. Being aware of these negative thoughts can assist you in changing your thinking to one that is a growth-oriented one. If you notice yourself looking at the things you're lacking when faced with a challenge it is a sign of a fixed-minded mindset. If you realize that you are fixated on the skills or knowledge you don't have You can make use of this as a basis for forming a plan to develop the knowledge or skills you don't have.

Change the way you think about these phrases can encourage your to challenge yourself to increase your abilities to learn and achieve the goals you want to accomplish. You can challenge these words by redefining the conversation you are having with yourself. Instead of dwelling on the fact that you don't have the necessary capabilities or expertise, tell yourself that you have the ability to develop and enhance your skills that will enable you to succeed in your objectives. Instead of dwelling on your mistakes or failing to achieve your goals, think about the fact that everyone makes mistakes and that even if you fail, you'll have learned many valuable lessons in the process.

It's an easy task to alter your internal dialogue to move towards a positive outlook but you can strengthen these beliefs more effectively by taking actions. If you want to believe that you're capable of growing and expanding and advancing, you must engage in actions that are supportive of the thoughts. Apply what you have said and set goals to collect more knowledge by reading more on a certain area, or set aside the time to practice the skills you'd like to master. Once you are acting according to your thinking Your mindset will change and motivate you to learn more.

Beliefs are formed as early as a child. It is common for us to not be aware of the positive or negative beliefs we have until later in the course of our lives. The beliefs you hold will make an enormous impact on all aspects of your life. They'll determine how you deal with those you interact with as well as the circumstances you confront.

What is the basis of belief?

Beliefs are the fundamental beliefs or ideas you make about your self and the world surrounding you. They can be re-enacted repeatedly throughout your life. We accept these beliefs as facts and presume they are accurate without considering where they came from or what factors contributed to their creation. They can affect how you see the world surrounding you. You can choose to develop a belief system that makes you feel confident, empowered and competent and confident, or you could create a belief system that make you feel cynical or defeated and causes you to feel inadequate and unimportant.

One thing one should realize is that the beliefs don't need to be fixed. The beliefs we hold as our foundational beliefs could be completely false and we are able to alter them! Examples of false beliefs:

* Everyone is more talented than me.

* I'm stupid.

Everyone is so selfish.

* Everybody takes advantage of me.

These beliefs can be deeply embedded in the way we live our lives. Our behavior or think and the way we feel are influenced by these fundamental beliefs. Your fundamental beliefs could be incorrect, but they are able to be altered. These beliefs can cause the need to be perfect and get the approval of people in our lives. When you are a teenager both of these elements can cause negative thoughts that can affect you for the rest of your life.

Perfectionism

The negative beliefs arise in the event that you feel like you're not enough. This kind of mindset could cause you to strive for better aspects of life. While striving to improve aspects of your life is a wonderful characteristic, having a perfectionism can lead to constant disappointments and failures. Perfection can cause you to feel like you're lower than others or unworthy to achieve what you want.

How you speak to yourself could help you discern if you're suffering from perfectionist views. Incessantly making comments like, "I should do better at schools," "I should have put more effort into my practice" and "I ought to have done something different in class" display a sloppy mindset. The words you make to yourself can make you believe that other people do not like the way you're acting or not working hard enough to be the best you can be.

Being a believer in perfection may cause feelings of isolated, having panic attacks, depression, and anxiety. This can make it difficult to establish and work towards the goals you would like to attain. People who have a strict belief system often do not feel at peace with themselves or think that people won't accept them as their unique qualities. It is likely that you will place more value on your accomplishments rather than your beliefs, and consequently, your self-worth could be diminished.

The need for approval

As a teenager As a teen, you'd like to be loved by your peers and surpass the expectations that your parents or teachers have put on you. It's normal to be accepted and loved However, the constant search to be liked can result in feelings of self-worth and anxiety, anger and frustration. When you begin to evaluate your self-worth in relation to how people like yourself, you'll start to have an unintentionally critical dialogue with yourself. You'll jump to conclusions and create lists after lists of the things you could say, could be doing, as well as the what you would have done. The constant desire for approval from others could put you feeling defense and, in turn, cause you to begin to turn people away from you.

There are people who will not love you or be your friend. Most times, it is in no way a result of any reason. There's no problem with this and there's nothing wrong with who you are. But this mindset of requiring approval from others will make you lose your self-image. You'll always be doing things or acting in a specific way because you believe that's how you can receive more praise from other people.

How your beliefs affect your thinking and act

Your beliefs will influence the way you behave in any situation. Your behavior will confirm your beliefs. If we believe negative things about ourselves, we be unable to feel worthy, unworthy and utterly terrible. If we form a belief that we hold about ourselves, then tend to immediately believe it to be true in every circumstance. The way we think about our beliefs is what we use to define individuals and things as positive or negative, or whether an event is hazardous or secure, or if our actions are acceptable or not. They are a major factor in determining whether our goals can be achieved or not.

We also have the ability to project our beliefs onto other people. The projections are based upon how we think others see us. If you're being intimidated, you could start to develop a impression that the bully is saying to you, and then begin to see yourself in the same way. In time, you'll begin to believe that all people you meet will be viewed the same way.

Beliefs are deeply embedded in every aspect of our lives. There are many beliefs that guide our actions thoughts, emotions, and thoughts. These beliefs can lead to thinking about our self and others who surround us. Certain thoughts help our well, however, they aren't based on factual information and may be a hindrance. The beliefs we hold are linked to your subconscious mind which is always seeking to confirm the beliefs. If we hold doubts or beliefs that are negative in our minds, we act and think in ways that further reinforces the beliefs.

When you believe in negative things and you are not aware of all evidence that contradicts your beliefs, and instead concentrate on the aspects that reinforce their beliefs. The beliefs we hold serve as filters. We look for what supports them and ignore what is in opposition to them. To change our beliefs, we must concentration on all evidence and not only those that support the beliefs that are unwelcome.

Find Your Fundamental Beliefs

Beliefs are formed as a result of a variety of reasons. The majority of teens develop the core beliefs they have based on their experience and how their parents behave towards them or with them. For instance, teenagers may form a core conviction about money that can be negative when they see their parents stressed about paying bills. Parents who continuously remind the children they love to remain vigilant can

40

create in their children the notion that our world is a dangerous environment or view everything as a threat. Both of these scenarios could cause youngsters to develop into teenagers and eventually adults who feel anxious.

Certain beliefs might have been formed in a child's form to be a good thing, but they won't ever serve you anymore as you grow older. For example children who grow in a family that is abusive might develop the belief that they're in power and the idea that standing up for their rights can only lead to more misery and they begin to believe that they're powerless. As the child matures and leaves the abusive environment the belief system is no longer helpful to them.

If you're trying to determine your most important beliefs, the first thing you should look is your mind. Your thoughts will help you identify patterns, and these themes could be the basis of your convictions. Try asking yourself these questions in order to discover your beliefs that are fundamental to you.

What aspects of your life could be influencing your convictions?

* What is the family dynamic of your family like?

What lessons did you take away from your early years?

* How do these lessons impact your perception of your world as well as the people you interact with and how you think about yourself?

Chapter 3: Setting Goals And How To Reach

These Goals

Goals with SMART

Why do you want to reach your target? What benefits will it bring? Answer this question or quit studying. This is one of your most powerful motivational factors.

S stands for specific

Your objective must be clear. The more precise your goal the better chance of being successful in achieving it. Consider for instance "I would like to shed some weight". However, I reply, "Ok that's great! What do you really want losing?"

"I would like to shed 15lbs." This is clearly more specific.

Here are a few additional examples of goals that are specific to the goal:

I can earn $100,000 per year through my business online.

I'll be driving an all-new Mercedes S Class.

I'll buy an apartment.

I'll shed 15 pounds.

I'll be in a lively healthy, positive relationship with someone I like, who I talk to in depth and who is curious.

Make it observable

To make sure that your plan is precise ensure that it is visible. You should make it clear you are able to observe your self doing what you are doing. One must be able to perceive the image. For instance, you might be able to imagine you driving a brand new Mercedes S Class, or visualize yourself walking into your brand new home or look at the $100,000 on your bank account or other statement, etc.

The Roadmap

Of course, making plans to accomplish this goal is crucial. It's like a map to get there. You have to begin from point A to get to the destination point B. However, between the two points, there might be detours, traffic, or stops that must be taken along the route. With a strategy you can arrange every step needed and set a timeline to determine when the tasks need to be completed to keep on the right track.

In the end, if you're constantly in the dark, and don't have a plan then you'll probably not succeed in achieving your desired outcome other than chance or luck or even you might succeed, but not even know that it was achieved.

If you have specific goals, each idea will have specific goals. If, for instance, you want to make more than $1,000 per month, you should create a checklist of the things you'll need to achieve to reach that goal. For those in the field of selling you'll need to reach out to 15 potential customers each day instead of 10. Perhaps you'll require 10 appointments every week instead of just 8. Set up a plan and establish specific dates and times for when you'll be doing this. For instance, on MWF I'll call between 1-5pm with two 20-minute breaks for lunch; on Tuesday and Thursdays, I'll schedule appointments with five people between 11am-7pm. It's all about sticking to being as precise as you can.

A different example is if you were trying to shed 10 pounds You could state, "To feel more attractive I'll shed 10 pounds over the course of 3 months by going to an exercise facility and working out MWF between 12pm and 1pm" And so on.

Language

Another crucial aspect is to select a words that are appealing to you since the language you choose to use can alter your perception of the goal. Words produce emotion. They can make you feel excited, or cause you to feel nothing whatsoever. The goal is making the conversation as engaging and engaging as it is.

Here's an exampleof "I can easily shed about 10 pounds in order to look more attractive, and weigh 150lbs at 13.3% bodyfat and I am totally enjoying this process." Other ideas you could consider could include "To be a more attractive body," or "To have more energy" or whatever is most effective for you, so you feel motivated and enthusiastic about your goals.

Step 2 2. Make Your Goal Specific. Take a look at the examples below and make your goals clear enough that anyone will understand what you're looking for. For instance, "To bring out my artistic side and generate money, I'll create an Photography Business."

M stands for Measurable.

The process of measuring something could seem simple and simple but it's actually the one that people experience the most trouble dealing with. If you don't take the time to measure it, how do you know if you've reached your goal How do you change your mind when you make a mistake so that you don't get stuck in a loop?

The goal you set should be something that you can track frequently. Many people make New Year's resolutions, but don't take the time to evaluate the progress or the regression which leaves them unfinished and ultimately neglected. Another reason why goals have to be clear is because you cannot quantify "I need to make more money" However, you can quantify "I would like to earn $1,000 per week."

The measurement of a goal provides tangible evidence of any growth or reduction. It can serve as an indicator of whether the goal has been met. The goal should be something you are able to evaluate frequently (e.g. weekly, bi-weekly). It is crucial to keep track of the progress and determine should be implemented.

Include it in your calendar you can set an alarm, so that when it sounds you must stop all activities and record your measurements to track the progress. To make the most of the process, you need to be able to measure your goals consistently to know the extent to which you're progressing. A weekly review or check-in is typically enough to assess what's working and what should be changed. It is impossible to measure "I would like be slimmer" however, you can gauge "I would like to shed 15 pounds over the course of 6 months."

We must measure our progress to be able to see improvements. It can be difficult to observe the changes from day to day because you're in the same place all day. It's like when you begin working out for a few weeks , and you don't appear any different, and then your friend asks, "Have you been working out? You're looking nice." You might have missed it that, but the person who asked noticed - that's a function that keeping track of your progress will perform.

If you're seeing results that are positive, you'll feel more inspired to work harder. By measuring your plan, you know when exactly you've achieved your goals. Then, you can be able to celebrate or reward yourself for your accomplishment.

Step3:

Create a SMART goal that is measurable If you've set it, "I will lose 15 pounds." When do you plan to finish it by? Do you want to break it down even further? For instance, if you say "I am going to lose fifteen pounds in four months" you could state, "Each week for the next six months , I will lose 1 pound a week." I'll happily exercise 3 times per week (treadmill 20 minutes and weights lifting thirty minutes).

A stands for Attainable

Your goal should be achievable. If you create an objective that is unattainable to achieve by yourself, you're setting yourself on the path to failure and are likely to be disappointed with your own. Therefore, let's make it achievable.

You can achieve almost every goal you can imagine if you organize your actions carefully Set a timeframe that permits you to complete the steps you need to take and make your goal sufficient to make it imperative that it be accomplished.

Step 4: Create Your SMART Goal attainable

A friend of mine taught me a fun and easy method to identify goals that are achievable. Here's her advice. Take out the pen and paper, and write down a list of things you are confident about yourself. Include your current strengths and skills. If this isn't something you are able to accomplish, you could ask someone in your family or a friend to list the most prominent positive traits.

Then, take a look at your objective and identify the qualities you'll be bringing into the equation to reach your goals. It is possible to base your 'what's attained' on past achievements, for example, any awards you received or other milestones you've achieved in your work.

Think about the characteristics you possess that can help you achieve your goal. For instance, you could think of, "Charm, Education, and Social/People Skills". Keep that document to keep a record of the abilities you possess and something you can refer to whenever you start doubting your abilities or give up on your goals.

GOAL:

_____

_____

My qualities that help me achieve this goal:

1.

_____

____

2.

_____

____

3.

_____

_____

4.

_____

_____

5.

_____

_____

R stands for Realistic

Your objective should be real. What is your plan of action? Do you plan to create an entirely new design of something? You could lose 5 pounds over one week? or buy a costly smartphone when you don't have any work. It's all feasible, but the biggest question is Are they realistic?

I suggest taking a big view. If you set an objective that's too far-fetched that you don't believe it's possible It could have negative results, including constantly giving yourself a hard time. Instead of feeling satisfied and fulfilled, you may be feeling less confident at yourself than you did previously.

Most of the time the plans that are realistic will be tangible. It is important to experience it using your senses, including smell, taste, sight as well as hearing and touch.

Things to Consider

Your current dreams could be achievable If you are determined to plan ahead and continue to push even when times are difficult. But, some of your desires might not be financially feasible right now So, you must devise a strategy to ensure it's financially feasible If you wish to achieve to do it enough. create a savings plan that will allow you to save money for it. Before you start working on the goal, it is important to take it apart and figure out whether it is a good idea for you.

If you want to get an ideal abs it is important to establish the proper timeline to ensure that your goal is achievable. If you're looking for more information about determining an achievable timeframe, there are a variety of health magazines to help you. You can also employ a personal trainer who will provide you with strategies to meet your fitness goals.

The Attainable and Realistic Rules go hand-in-hand. If your goals aren't achievable, they may not be feasible. The issue is that there are aspects that may be achievable for some people, but not for others. Be honest in determining if your objective is achievable.

For example, if you want spending more time in your family rather than going out or working with your friends it is likely that you will need be able to tell "no" to many more things in order to have "family quality time". If you're certain that you're not able to (or can't spend less time with your friends) and you are not able to, then it's not an achievable goal in the event that you're not willing to sacrifice other things (such as a shorter sleep schedule, or perhaps fewer activities outside of school) to find a time for family time.

If you're struggling to decide whether or not it's feasible then consider asking a relative or friend. Additionally, I would not recommend asking someone who is pessimistic in their outlook because they'll probably block your dream completely. Therefore, you should ask a reliable and optimistic, neutral person.

Step 5 5. Make Your Goal SMART Reliable

Answer these questions:

* Does it fit into your daily routine?

Do you have the time each week to make your plan successful?

Have you got the money to get started?

* Do you have expertise or knowledge?

Do you have the drive and determination to go the extra mile to achieve this?

If you answer "No" for these queries, it's crucial to modify or rethink your goals.

T stands for Timeline

To be completed, it has to be completed on time or with an established timeline. The goal must be supported by a time-frame. If there isn't a time frame, there is no sense of urgency. If you're looking to lose 10 pounds. What date do you intend to shed it.

Are you using an on-wall calendar or a flipbook calendar that you can use to record your progress and remind you of deadlines? Do you have sticky notes in your bedroom or office?

If your strategy is based upon a 10 to 20-year process If you do, you could have difficulties making your plan a reality and it's likely to shift (which is normal). However, with time, it may be difficult to continue pushing forward since it's far from the horizon.

The way to meet the goal of achieving distant targets is by breaking them in smaller parts. For instance, if you set an objective to have five millions dollars in your account within 10 years, then the goal must break it down into small pieces (e.g. five-year plans and a 1-year plan, a 1 month plan, etc.). The goals that are less invasive like a week, 1 month or even one year are easier to visualize than the 10 years down road.

Make it urgent

Consider the impact of the power of a deadline. For example as a student at school, you were under the requirement to complete the assignment, or else you could face consequences, such as detention after school or a failing mark, that would force you to take a new course , or perhaps be expelled from the school.

You're looking to create pressure on yourself to finish it completed. Make yourself feel more urgent.

The possibility of having consequences for failing to achieve the goal may be a powerful incentive to overcome barriers.

If, for instance, you fail to reach your goal within the date, what do you do to create an unpleasant discomfort? Do you donate $500 to your neighbor , or an organization or homeless man in the streets? If you make a commitment to this for each goal you set Imagine the number of goals you can achieve!

Step 6: Establish the SMART Goal you have set a timeline and make it urgent!

What is the most realistic timeframe you are able to commit to reaching Your SMART Goal? Set a date (and urgent) to your goals, for example, "I will lose 15 pounds in four weeks (by the 31st of July). If I fail then I have to make a donation of $100 to the person next to me in Starbucks in the next (fill in an exact date).

The Reasons Why You (and everyone else on the planet) requires Smart Goals!

Life can be messy, chaotic and stress-inducing. There is no doubt about that. On some days, you might awake thinking about all the tasks you have to do today, and then think there's no way that you'll ever complete everything! Stress can be created, and the most important thing is the way you decide to apply it.

Do you utilize it to boost your energy levels and keep you motivated to complete tasks at greater speed than usual?

Do you find yourself using anxiety as an excuse to complain, feel bad for yourself and lie in bed, doing little done? If this is the case Here's a useful approach.

It's a shift in perspective strategy that addresses one of the questions below:

Who are the people you admire?

One example could be the person you love (mom or father), Richard Branson, Tony Robbins

If someone were in front of you this moment, what could that person tell you to do?

Use this as motivation and inspiration to get yourself up and engaged!

Habits

If your life isn't what you would like it to be It will remain as it is until you decide to make the make a change. When you have decided what you would like to change, you can take daily small steps for 30 days until it is the norm and is comfortable. For instance, if are looking to reduce the body fat percentage and you be planning to workout each day at M, W, F, and take a walk of 2 miles on off days. If you follow this routine for a period of 30 days, it's likely to be a routine. In reality, if you were to do this for a period of 30 days, you'll be strange to not workout during those days, particularly when you're seeing results, like what it feels when you don't clean your teeth at night (or early in the morning).

Another example could be writing a book for one hour per day (which is the way I came up with this book) or doing your work for an hour every day, or visiting an espresso bar to meet two new people for an hour each day to build a connect or establish an exciting new partner - doing every day for 30 days in order to build a habit.

Comfort Zone

One of the biggest obstacles to achieve the goal is not just making changes to your habits, but also taking a step beyond your comfortable zone. It is the place you feel the most comfortable but it offers only little benefits. Moving out the comfort zones is where you'll discover massive growth and achieve your goals. It's fascinating to discover what happens when you're uncomfortable, and discover the things you can accomplish.

For instance, I finally found the confidence to speak with people I believed were intimidating, for example...the gorgeous woman, the professional, or our rich intimidating boss. When I changed my perception through NLP my life totally changed. These people were at the same level with me, and I was comfortable and encouraged to speak with them.

Chapter 4: Real-Life Challenges And

Strategies For Managing Positively Daily

Challenges

How can you increase the chances that you'll be able to respond positively in the future?

There are numerous effective treatments you can employ to treat your anxiety and depression. But the best part is there's methods you can pick to try to increase your chance of coping with situations in a positive manner.

One of these strategies is:

Practicing positive self-assurance

The first thing to recognize is that anxiety can make you focus on every negative thing that happens throughout your day. That is, instead of focusing on ways to utilize your power to perform positive things, you think about how you failed to handle situations in the correct way. The issue with this type of mindset is that it could quickly become a destructive mental process that can create depression and anxiety worse than they already are.

To avoid negative thoughts, it's crucial to shift your focus to the positively oriented aspects in your daily life. This means thatif you begin to fret about situations that aren't working out, you should change your focus to positive things going on instead. In school, you might be feeling a bit down about the last time you spoke to your teacher or classmates. But instead of dwelling on the things that didn't go as planned Try to think of the interactions that went well and learn from them in order to improve your next interactions.

Keep a journal of your anxiety

If you're depressed or anxious, there's one thing certain: it's difficult to pinpoint what's the reason for the symptoms. To figure this out it is crucial to keep a diary of your experiences. When you are feeling anxious make a note of the factors that make you feel this way. Make sure you record your emotions, feelings and even your actions.

It is true that simply recording your thoughts and anxieties and worries, you can deal with certain situations that make you be overwhelmed. Revisiting your journal when you are feeling stressed or bring it up in CBT sessions plays an important role in helping you examine the main causes of your anxiety , so you can ultimately work through the issues.

Refusing negative thoughts

Recognize that if you focus on positive thoughts, you will effortlessly overcome negative thoughts whenever you are experiencing anxiety attacks. A fear of negative consequences could take over your life. If you find the negative thought process creeping into your mind and you are struggling, do all you can to imagine positive outcomes you could achieve from your circumstances for example, a vacation adventure.

For example, if you're scared of heights and frequently experience nausea, sweating and a higher heart rate, instead of thinking about your worries, focus on the positives that could happen from your travels and the activities you've scheduled to do during your journey. Consider your surroundings as beautiful area you're going to and the gorgeous people you're eager to meet. So, you can quickly switch your focus away off of negative events.

The process of setting up the routine

Have you ever thought that establishing an established routine can assist you in getting through your daily routine with ease? It's the only factor that can help reduce the chance of experiencing unanticipated triggers to your anxiety. The process of setting up a routine can ensure that everything you have set out to complete is completed at the time you finish the day. This ensures that no task is left unfinished, thereby less anxiety.

It is essential to incorporate nutritious meals and regular exercises to ensure your physical and mental health are well-nourished. If you have a plan for your day-to-day tasks, your mind will be shifted to the daily schedule and the little victories that happen throughout the day meaning that you do not have to be worried about the uncertainties that your day might bring.

Practicing relaxation techniques

The way to relax varies from individual to the next. This is due to the fact that every person finds their inner peace during various actions. It is good to know that there's a broad variety of methods can be used to help calm your anxieties. Some of these methods include yoga, deep breathing, and meditation.

Through deep breathing, you will effortlessly ease the tension and agitation that's taking you down in the tummy. Close your eyes and pay focus to your breathing. Breathe deeply to your diaphragm. Feel the anxiety disappear.

Another method is to use yoga and meditation to help ward away anxiety. These methods have a relaxing and relaxing effect, mainly due to similar to music, they redirect your focus from the things that are the cause of your anxiety and instead focus on yourself and the wonderful things life offers. Then, you'll start feeling calm and relaxed.

Inspiring yourself to exercise

It is among the most essential aspects of living a healthy life. It is because it offers both mental and physical health advantages. When you incorporate the exercise routine into your day you will be in awe and motivated to achieve it! You'll be determined to reach your goals every day, regardless of what obstacles are in your path. This is what can shift your focus away on your anxiety and redirect the energy into positive outcomes.

Practice acceptance

You must realize that there will be circumstances in your life that will beyond your control. Sometimes, these events could cause you to become nervous. Beating this anxiety, fear and worry can be difficult, particularly with the thought of being in the unknown. But, the truth is, if you choose to dwell about the unknowable, it is not going to assist you in making adjustments.

It is best to recognize the situations that cause anxiety and discover if they are within your control. If so, it is essential to determine the tasks that can aid in getting rid of anxiety and stress and begin to tackle these tasks. If you're able to say no then it is essential to recognize that there are times when nothing in our lives is under our control. Remember that there are some situations aren't yours to alter and that's perfectly acceptable.

The most effective way to spot the root of your problems and problems is to do it immediately.

The first thing to be aware of is that anxiety disorders are not easily identified. It is because there is a high level of excitation from anxiety-related worries that affect character traits. As we age it is common to see the experience of headaches, fatigue and GIT anxiety. The worst part is that anxiety-related disorders typically occur in conjunction with other conditions that cause symptoms like those associated with anxiety. Because of these concomitant disorders that detection and identification may be quite a hassle.

The primary distinction between normal worry and anxiety is the perception of distress and capacity to perform. While serious anxiety typically affects one's functioning however, there's a good possibility that mild anxiety will not be obvious until you use CBT with a trained therapist who can seek out more details.

It is crucial to inform your therapist of the various aspects that might be causing you to worry. The truth isthat symptoms of anxiety disorder are inconsistent and painful fear as well as the conflict between what's believed to be real and reality.

One of the ways you can pinpoint your issues are:

Physical complaints

As older adults are more likely to have physical symptoms of anxiety The most common symptoms to look for include chest pains, and shortness of breath. They are extremely important since they are often a sign of medical conditions , and it is crucial to pinpoint the cause.

Food habits

If you're stressed there is a good possibility that you'll begin experiencing eating disorder. Also you might be prone to eating excessively to reduce stress, and thus becoming overweight. However you could eat less and then lose weight.

Sleep patterns

If you're anxious there is a high possibility that your sleeping patterns could be affected. A lot of people are reluctant to sleep to keep their worries at bay. Others might stay up all night thinking of dangerous scenarios or fears so that they don't have bad night visions.

Other interests and interests

A lot of people with depression or anxiety tend to avoid things that were once enjoyable. They are able to do less activities they take satisfaction from as they're more afraid.

They also prefer to stay at home to keep from having to face their anxieties. Actually, due to the lack of any activities that allow them to relax and distract their minds from the stress and worries and worries, they are more likely to use drugs and other illicit substances. It is because they are trying to stay in constant fear.

Social isolation

This is among the most prominent signs of depression and anxiety. When I say the word "social isolation," I don't mean being a lonely person. It is simply a matter of being isolated from the the world. You might be living on your own however, if you are surrounded by friends, have a night out with them and enjoy a range of things to engage in when you have time, then you're perfectly well.

The term "socially isolated is a term used to describe people who have lost their connections, human touch and contact with friends and families. They are also not involved in any activities or hobbies that are of interest to them. Apart of going out to go grocery shopping their only option to interact with them is to visit their therapy.

There are a variety of reasons individuals become socially lonely. For some , it's due to certain physical issues, while some are unable to socialize because they're scared to leave their home. Most often, they get being trapped in a vicious circle.

If you're this kind of person, you need be aware that limiting yourself won't help you solve your problem. This means that you require assistance. Social activities and interactions are a few of the things that can lift your spirits, lift you up and soothe your worries.

Don't let your worry, anxiety and anxieties to take the top of you. Don't allow your fear to erase the most enjoyable aspects as well as years. Instead of locking yourself in your house and beggar yourself from dawn until sunset take a moment to consider the things that can help you the most. Take a moment to think about what you're not getting.

Afraid of yourself will keep your thoughts in isolation and , consequently, cause more depression and anxiety. The vicious cycle of isolation can be difficult however, you must be prepared, willing and able to extend your hand to those surrounding you and seek assistance from those who are the most important to you including your family and your friends.

How to stay clear of "black and white" thinking, distortions of your thinking, and generalization of the population

There are a variety of ways to overcome cognitive distortions. This can be achieved through various techniques and exercises that can help you change your negative thinking pattern into an optimistic way of thinking. This includes such activities as:

Reflection on your thoughts

Self-assessment is a skill you will never be wrong when you don't get caught up in self-judgment. This is due to the fact that whenever you observe cognitive distortions in your mind, you could decide to acknowledge these by becoming more aware of them.

One method of achieving this is to keep the notes of these thoughts to look at the similarities or differences between the two. It is important to realize that there is no reason to believe that you're not fortunate. It is your responsibility to justify these beliefs and to stop them each time they arise.

Do you have a question?

Although you might not be used to examining yourself, it's vital to exercise this option frequently. If you ask yourself questions about your opinions, you are making sure it's not based on cognitive distortions. This will ensure that you do not believe misconceptions regarding the various situations that you come across.

Listen to the opinions of others.

If you take the time to hear the opinions of others and gain their perspectives on life it is expanding your perspective on life. In the end, you'll be able to allow those mental distortions to go away, and you will be able to see the world with a more objective perspective.

Find information from trustworthy sources

Before you start blame others or yourself for mistakes make sure you compare your information with as many trustworthy sources as you can. This is one way by to avoid causing catastrophe in circumstances.

Develop a critical mindset

When it comes to anxiety related, one thing you should keep in your mind is that it's always a good idea to consider more critically. If you do this, you will notice that your view of situations will become more holistic. This means that you aren't allowing you to be swept in the midst of obvious facts. So, whenever something happens instead of leaping to conclusions it is better to look at the pros and cons of a particular action before making an informed decision.

Get advice from your beloved ones

The majority of the time, it is easy to become distracted by the circumstances and mental distortions. Instead of allowing this to happen, it's crucial to tackle every circumstance with someone you are able to trust. In this way, you will gain a fresh perspective and ensure that you're impartial.

It isn't difficult to overcome cognitive distortions. But, one thing you must never overlook is the amount of discomfort these reasoning errors cause and you should try as hard as you can to feel for your fellow sufferers and those who are suffering from similar issues. It is true that anyone has anxiety issues at any moment. If you are constantly critical of yourself or other people this can increase stress or anger that likely cause the problem to get worse.

Here are some useful suggestions you can consider to prevent cognitive distortions

There is a way to alter your thinking

The painful situations we encounter every day have the potential to alter the person we are. Some instances could be worse , and they are difficult to remove from minds However, it is important to be aware that you cannot alter things that have occurred over the years. You are able to choose to take an entirely different mindset to approach scenarios in a different way when you come to them in the near future.

Eliminating cognitive distortions is a process that requires dedication, determination and perseverance. Each time you experience thoughts of negative thoughts running through your mind, try to counter it by presenting a positive argument that is in opposition to the idea. If you do this, you'll end with a positive perspective.

Watch your language

What we say and how we express ourselves verbally determines the quality of our thoughts and actions. It affects our opinions. It's easy to become involved in words that are negative and demeaning. This can cause more harm. Instead of using negative language instead, try to use positive words, those that convey optimism instead of a negative outlook. If you can change the way you speak you'll start to believe that you are competent, thus improving your overall health and outlook.

Develop mental health habits that are healthy and positive.

Mental health and wellbeing are important as physical health. Both are crucial to ensure your health and wellbeing is in full. Certain practices will guarantee that you're taking good treatment of yourself, and you're protecting your mind from things that could be harmful and destructive.

Instead of dwelling on the things that didn't go as planned build an emotional and interpersonal intelligence. Don't try to be something you're not. Be aware of the person you are, so that you can fill your soul by what you can do to improve. Take care of your diet, get some rest and always work on your mental abilities. Make sure that no matter what the situation might be, you participate in activities that are enjoyable for you.

Do you realize that self-esteem makes you feel confident, and therefore is the most important factor to ensuring mental well-being? If you don't believe in yourself, there's no way that other people can be confident in your self-esteem. The good thing is that there are many ways you can apply to boost self-esteem. Some of these strategies include:

Self-limiting beliefs are pushed aside

Sometimes, our thoughts are similar to the thoughts of the child. We believe that we are able to take on the world. When we are involved in the adult world and realize that our hopes, passions and ideas are crushed. That's when people around us try to impose their views on us. They determine what we are able to do and can't do with our lives , and it can be a bit difficult!

Instead of being entangled in what others want to see in your life, it's essential that you set your own personal limits. The best method to do this is to place yourself in different situations. That is you should not be within someone else's picture of your life. Instead, embrace the fearful. This can not only help you boost your self-esteem, but it will also increase your confidence and gain a new perception of your self. In reality, you will be amazed by what you can achieve!

Do not mix memory with facts

It is important to grasp that memory doesn't store information the same way we are presented with it. Human nature drives us to glean the essence of an entire event or event and store the data in ways that are logical to us. This is the reason people who are witness to the same incident frequently have very distinct interpretations of the identical.

Chapter 5: Learning How To Learn And

Approach The Schooling Process With A

Different Mentality

Cognitive Behavioral Therapy is the type of therapy focused on how your perceptions and interpretations of the world affect your general behavior. CBT assists you in understanding how your emotions, thoughts and beliefs impact your behavior.

If you're recovering from brain injury CBT is utilized to deal with your negative beliefs, which can develop following the injury, and can impact recovery and rehabilitation.it can also be used to deal with negative thought patterns that you may have been experiencing prior to the TBI. Negative thoughts can impede the recovery process.

In CBT, you're expected to spot illogical and abnormal behaviors that are triggered by false beliefs. These behavior patterns can be detrimental to healing. Then, you are encouraged to modify these behaviors by altering your thinking patterns. Moreover,

CBT requires that you play an active part in your recovery. You will be given homework assignments that will assist you during the recovery journey.

Furthermore, you're required to keep track of your behavior. This allows you to be aware of your behaviour patterns and allows you to become more responsible in changing your behavior for faster recovery.

Effectiveness of CBT for individuals with Acute Brain Injuries (TBI)

The efficacy of CBT in treating TBI patients is contingent on the level of your cognitive function. The following are some personal characteristics that you need to have for the purpose of undergoing Rational Emotive Behavioral Therapy (REBT) A type used in Cognitive Behavioral Therapy that is efficient in treating TBI patients.

You should be patient and adaptable when dealing with tension and anger.

It is also important to be willing to accept the possibility of uncertainty.

You must have self-acceptance qualities and be able to accept non-urtopianism.

The use of REBT for those suffering from TBI is highly advised. Therapists are encouraged to share REBT strategies to TBI patients more flexible and collaboratively. They should be flexible to the requirements of their patients instead of the patients' changing to TBI. Additionally sessions of REBT must be designed in a unique manner. Sessions should be repeated and structured in order to cater to the requirements of TBI individuals.

How CBT can be used to help TBI individuals.

The use of behavior therapy is highly advised as an intervention to alter the behavior of people suffering from TBI. This treatment method can help you re-learn important skills, such as self-care, in order to heal from your injuries as quickly as possible. It's also been proven that CBT enhances the quality of life for those who suffer from persistent post concessional symptoms. PCS are common in people who suffer from brain injuries.

In a research conducted in collaboration with Dr. Potter Sebastian, Institute of

Psychiatry, Psychology, and Neuroscience in London to assess the efficacy of an individualized CBT treatment and found that CBT results in improved quality of life for people who suffer from RBI. It was also found that CBT can be effective for treating secondary issues that result from TBI that result from TBI, like anxiety and fatigue.

Important Characteristics of the Therapy

There is a set of guidelines that therapists could follow to ensure that they have productive sessions with TBI patients. The guideline includes:

1. Participation by TBI patients in the idea and concept of the program. Patients should also be involved in the execution in the course. The patients should be motivated to take part so as to feel inspired to participate in the therapy sessions. Participation by the patients makes them feel part of the therapy program.

2. The objectives and goals of the program need to be clearly stated and clearly stated before sessions begin. The therapist collaborates with the patient to come up

the clear goals and objectives for the course.

3. The therapist must also assist the patient to identify the negative behavior that is hindering an effective recovery plan. A positive response to replace the negative behaviour is identified and clearly identified. The therapist will then aid the patient in reaffirming this positive characteristic which can speed up recovery.

4. The plan must be constructed in a positive manner. Positive changes that are reported by the patient must be rewarded and encouraged. The therapist should congratulate the patient for every try to make a alter their behavior. The patient's efforts to changes should be greatly aided.

5. Feedback from patients is a good thing and should be strongly recommended. Patients are encouraged to provide promptly feedback to the Therapist.

The use of CRT to promote Brain Recovery

Cognitive issues pose a major problem for people suffering from brain injuries. The resulting difficulties create an enormous obstacle in a healthy recovery and getting back to normal. Brain injury sufferers tend to be afflicted by issues with the social and emotional aspects of their lives as well as safety judgement, and they may also have difficulties when planning and executing the future actions. The injury can affect your ability to look after yourself, maintain appointments, accomplish tasks and also to be a regular participant in others in your community.

Treatment is required for these cognitive issues in order to live a good health and avoid damaging consequences. One one of the most effective treatments for your situation can be Cognitive Rehabilitation Therapy (CRT). CRT incorporates a variety of strategies to address and treat the symptoms.

CRT's Approaches

There are two ways to CRT:

1. It aims to improve the cognitive system's ability to perform efficiently when confronted with different tasks.

2. Compensatory treatment helps an individual offer solutions to a specific issue. One can master self-curing techniques.

Health Care Providers for CRT

CRT provides a broad range of licensed health professionals. These include:

* Nurses

* Physical therapy

* Neuropsychologists

Counselors for vocational rehabilitation

* Occupational therapy

* Physicians

* Where can you locate CRT-related services

* Hospitals

* Inpatient rehabilitation units for community

* Rehabilitation for brain injury units

* Outpatient departments

* Hospitals

CRT treatments can be performed in various formats. This includes:

* Day program for treatment

* Individual therapy

* Group therapy

Cognitive Exercises That Help those suffering from TBI

There are a variety of exercises you can make use of to enhance and protect your cognitive ability after suffering a brain injury. The exercises will also improve your cognitive abilities. The brain needs continuous practice for it to function effectively. Exercise can also help your brain to keep it healthy and enhance its health.

In the event that you trigger your body via activities, more neurons are stimulated. These neurons allow the body to function at its highest levels. Exercise is more crucial when you have suffered an injury to the brain. Exercise stimulates your neuroplasticity which helps your brain reset itself to normal.

There are a variety of cognitive exercises that will stimulate and test the brain's ability to process information in various ways, so that it can create new neural patterns of thinking. They also help to strengthen cognitive abilities like recall and memory, which you lost following an injury to your brain. The exercises you can do include:

Exercises to improve attention and concentration for people with TBI

These exercises can help you multi-task. The brain learns to pay attention to multiple tasks. This includes:

1. Letters and numbers

The person who assists you reads the names of people in an unmistakable voice. It is crucial that they read out the numbers in a slow rate. When you read the number and you write them down each one at a time. You may also write down the numbers you have heard in a list that is provided prior to the reading.

2. A Rhythmic Matching

The person taps the rhythmic sounds on a desk with his hands. When they tap to the beat, pay attention attentively and try to replicate the sound you hear. When the exercise is progressing as the participant taps the rhythms must try to work at a quicker rate and may create more intricate rhythmic patterns.

If you are urged to choose any two-digit number, the number you choose is added to the figure three times. Then, subtract seven from the total number. Repeat this process repeatedly using various figures including subtraction, addition and addition. This exercise is beneficial because your brain is focused on holding many details at a time.

Additionally, you'll increase the brain's capacity to organize and process information.

3. Excellent Motor skills

This is a fantastic method to enhance your brain's abilities following the trauma to your brain. These include:

* puzzles with jigsaws

* Therapy putty exercise

* stacking pennies

* rubber bands that stretch

* studying to play an instrument, such as the piano

4. Relaxing outside while you update your journal

When you go outside and write down whatever that you can hear, see or smell, the part of your brain which is normally not active is occupied. This will allow you focus better. If you're having trouble writing because of your injuries, you may request someone else to write for you while you read your thoughts out.

To make this exercise successful, you must be aware of your surroundings

5. Improve Your Problem-Solving Ability

Being unable to resolve issues in your life could make you be overwhelmed by the prospect of anxiety. people who are struggling with problem-solving skills frequently feel lacking confidence when exploring new ideas or participating in risky activities due to the fear that, should something go wrong, they won't have the knowledge to respond. The uncertainty that comes with it could lead to fears of being at risk with no skills necessary to make it through even though the majority of scenarios do not pose a threat to life. When this is the case anxiety can develop. It is normal. As anxiety begins to grow it becomes difficult to take on new challenges because fear of being vulnerable and lacking the abilities to safeguard yourself. If you continue to avoid any new activities due to the fear of being vulnerable, it could cause depression which could further affect the mental well-being.

The process of improving your ability to solve problems means you are equipped with the ability to deal with challenging situations, so that you do not feel an overwhelming feeling of vulnerability when you go through these situations. In essence, you develop confidence in yourself as well as the ability to endure whatever challenges you face. One of the best ways to develop your problem-solving capabilities is engaging in logic-based games or puzzles. These games, such as Sudoku or riddles were created to get you started thinking about the problem in a way you can figure out the answer to the the issue. Engaging in these problems-solving games is an excellent method to improve your ability to tackle challenges. This will help you be more confident in your problem-solving skills. Mindfulness can also be a beneficial practice for problem-solving because it shows you to detach from the emotional reactivity to be able to evaluate situations with a rational state of mind. In bringing yourself back to rational thinking can improve your decision-making abilities and ability to think through problems. This allows you to deal with challenges in your daily life with a more logical view.

Utilizing Mantras and Meditation

Mantras and meditation are an excellent option to boost your mental wellbeing by aiding you in improving your concentration while giving you more free from negative or intrusive thoughts. Mantras, or personal mantras can be a fantastic method to boost your self-confidence and help you see things in a more positive optimistic, confident, and positive viewpoint. Your mantra could be whatever you want to make it, as long as it helps you in feeling confident and inspired to face any obstacles you encounter in your daily life. You may also alter your mantra, or choose several if you believe that you require more strength throughout your life.

It is possible to repeat your mantra whenever you require extra support when facing challenges within your life. You can also repeat it during meditation in order to reinforce the mantra within your mind, so that it becomes more powerful when you apply it regularly in your daily life. Mantra-based meditations may involve sitting in a quiet place and repeating your mantra repeatedly over to yourself. Or, you can just repeat your mantra quietly to yourself in your head and allow yourself to be overwhelmed by the strength of the mantra.

The act of meditation itself is useful. While meditating along with mantras is extremely effective but meditative practice on its by itself can enhance your mindfulness and assist you in achieving a greater sensation of peace within your daily life. On the mindfulness side it allows you to be more aware of the kind of thoughts you are having within your mind and what they could be creating a feeling. It is important to be aware of the thoughts and emotions, without trying to evaluate them or alter their effects in any fashion. Instead, you must be aware of them in order that you gain an understanding of the inner workings of you in that moment. From a perspective of relaxation it is possible to relax and find peace with everything around you, this allows the ability to "offload" everything that might cause you to feel overwhelmed or overwhelmed. The more you practice meditation your mind, the less stress you carry around and, in turn, makes future stress-inducing situations less difficult for you to bear.

Relaxing in the Healing Nature's benefits Nature

Nature's healing properties have a profound influence on human beings. Although we've boxed ourselves in our homes and have surrounded ourselves in cement, and limited the vast majority of our natural habitat to gardens or designated forests We still seek out nature to be at the center of us. Being in contact with nature any moment can have a profound positive effect on your health. Nature can help you free your mind from the stress and bustle of everyday life and be immersed in an entire ecosystem in which the motto is "let let it go" since everything can do as it wills at any moment. There is a lot to learn from nature and also plenty of healing can be achieved in its presence.

Forest bathing and tree-hugging can be thought to be two beneficial practices to aid the process of overcoming mental stress and experiencing a sense peace within your daily life. Bathing in the forest, or simply taking a walk in the forest, lets you sit in a tranquil and peaceful place, and observe the world unfold all around you. When you are in the woods, there's no agenda, no sense of time, or the urgent necessity to complete anything. Instead the forest is focused on being in the present moment and living in peace with the people surrounding you. If you are able to hug the trees you see in the forest, you can take this opportunity to take a moment and physically connect with an incredibly peaceful creatures in the forest. Trees can offer a lot in terms of studying mindfulness since they live their entire lives only focusing on growing towards the sun and staying tall in their own place. Trees don't walk or run, nor do they crawl. They remain stationary for all their lives growing up in only one place. Relaxing in the slow, concentrated nature of the forest for a short time can help you to remember that not everything needs to be quick and some of the greatest things that happen in life are the result of the slowest and most insignificant efforts.

Another method to be in touch with nature is by bird watching. Bird watching is extremely peaceful however it also lets you be aware. While watching birds, you need to be quiet and still to ensure that you don't worry about attracting birds away. The ability to be calm and patient is necessary, which will allow you to discover how to sit comfortably and relax surrounding you while the birds you are watching lead their lives. Furthermore, the simple feeling of watching the animals live their lives with no any worries or tension is an excellent method to recollect the real value of life and bring peace to your thoughts.

In the end, if you'd like to go outside and engage in it physically gardening can be a wonderful activity that is both relaxing and productive. Gardening itself lets you get away from the normal world and concentrate to something that is more relaxing and slower. You can concentrate your attention in tilling the soil or planting seeds or gardening, watering the garden, pulling out weeds or just keeping an eye on the garden to ensure that everything is flourishing. When you're in your garden, it is possible to are able to commit to this time paying close the garden, and the things that are happening in your garden. Furthermore, by having your garden, you're staying productive, by teaching yourself to remain focused and reach long-term goals with success. Gardening requires patience, time and perseverance and these are three mental habits that can transform your mental world in the process of mastering the art of overcoming depression, anxiety and other mental problems. When you continue to garden and weeding, you'll begin to reap the benefits of your work with healthy plants that will grow with your help and allow you to feel fulfilled and fulfilled.

Finding value in feeling small

One of the primary reasons people suffer from depression or anxiety is because they feel inadequate. Being apathetic can be exhausting difficult, emotional, and even uncomfortable. Sometimes, feeling inadequate may make you feel unimportant and feeling like there's nothing to be proud of because you're not significant enough to be worth it. However it's not the case but the sensations of being insignificant can cause people to believe that's the situation.

If you're interested in stopping suffering from feeling small, you should begin to see the value in being small. Being small can make you feel inadequate or be viewed as an opportunity to release yourself from the burden of the world you've been carrying on your shoulders.

If you are feeling personally responsible for resolving all the problems in the world and helping everyone else in your life be happier or more successful at things, feeling inadequate can make you believe that you're not capable of fulfilling your goal.

Chapter 6: Illustrations, Application

Question And Exercises

It is essential that parents and children collaborate to overcome negative thoughts, manage emotions, and modify behaviours in a coordinated manner. If you are working with your child to understand the things they struggle with, often you'll notice that you've been struggling with the same issues also. The exercises and techniques that are included in this book are perfect for parents and their children to work on together. Each one of these activities will aid your child in developing the abilities needed to manage their emotions, counter negative thoughts, and regulate how they react to situations that are overwhelming.

Make sure you listen to your child's questions. It is also crucial to be honest and transparent with your child about the ways you have been struggling or struggled with the issues they're facing. Be sure to provide your child with the love and support they need and show patience. A lot of these activities can be immediate and impact your child's behavior. Other exercises must be practiced frequently to help your child master the tools in their own way.

Recognizing emotions

We have discussed a few ways to assist your child in recognizing emotions. For instance, ask them what they feel when watching an episode on TV or reading the book. It is also possible to have your child draw emotions' faces, and discuss the reason why they chose to draw the faces in that manner to express the emotion. Games that you play around the house could be utilized for helping your children be able to understand emotions.

Emotions Candy Land

If you're playing Candy Land or the Chutes and Ladders board game, you can identify a particular emotion or feeling to each color by the table (yellow for joy and red for love and anger, green for jealousy and orange for gratitude) You can play the game as you normally would , but every time they touch one of the colors, they have to recall a time they felt this way. It is also possible to have them describe what they would have done to cause someone else to feel this way, or describe what they feel and what they could take to make to feel better when they are feeling the way they do.

Emotions Jenga

You can purchase a smaller Jenga set in the majority of dollar stores instead of having a bigger version. Paint the small circles on each of the blocks to signify an emotion (red means love; yellow for happiness blue for sadness and red for anger) You can choose any colors you prefer and assign each emotion. The game can be played in the same way you would normally. Every time a block is pulled, either you or your child must describe a moment when you felt the emotion that is correlated with the color of the block. You may also ask your child talk about the emotion and ask how they could make them feel better should they feel a negative emotion.

Regular Jenga is an excellent game that helps with anxiety. It helps children to become more at ease with their anxious emotions and help them remember that their fears aren't going to cause harm to them. The anxiety that builds in anticipation of blocks to be thrown over is an important aspect that can be utilized to help your child learn about anxiety.

Indoor basketball

You can make an easy basketball hoop with the laundry basket or garbage bin. Crush into a few pieces of paper into balls. You and your child could play around trying to put the barber in the basket. If you succeed in getting the paper into the basket the basket, you will earn two points. If you miss, you must answer a question. If you can answer the correct answer, you will earn one point. Questions should be written on index cards, and should focus on the various emotions. Some sample questions can include:

What is it that you mean to be feeling (happy sad, angry or concerned)?

* If I'm (mad or sad, anxious,) What is the something I can do to make me feel better?

* My body is feeling tight and hot when I feel?

* If I'm angry I should scream or shout. False or true?

* If I'm unhappy, I should speak to someone about the things that bother me. True or false?

I'm feeling relaxed and happy, what are my feelings?

It is possible to share stories and ask questions regarding how they feel and what they can do to improve their mood or what they could do differently to make them feel better.

You could set a goal to achieve the number of points you have to accumulate before the game ends. For children younger than 10 it is possible to declare that the first player who scores 5 or 10 points is the winner and for the older kids, who score 20 or more points.

Techniques for breathing

Instructing your child in a variety of breathing techniques can allow them to instantly to calm their mind and body when they face something they are afraid of. These breathing techniques can reduce heart rate and help your child to take control of their emotions. They can be employed in any environment as well. They should practice often and not just in times when you notice your child suffering from some unpleasant feeling.

* Starfish breathing

Let your child stand with arms spread out toward their sides. Take an exhale while they lift their arms over their heads. After exhaling, have them return their arms down towards their side.

* Blowing bubbles

It is possible to provide your child with real bubbles to blow or make them play blowing bubbles using the wand of their imagination. Practice taking a deep breath to ensure that air fills up their stomachs, and let them exhale slowly. If you're using bubbles, tell that the more slowly they exhale, the larger the bubble will get. You can then have them pop the bubbles while they contemplate negative thoughts or feelings they experience to help release the negative thoughts from their minds.

* Counting

Your child can breathe in for a period of five before exhaling for five counts. You could also ask them to hold their hands before them and make use of their pointer finger to trace out the outline of their fingers. When they run their fingers up the the opposite hand, they should inhale. as they slide their finger down the side of their finger that is on the other hand the exhale.

Impulse Control

There are many games which will help your child learn the ability to control their impulses without being aware of. After you have finished playing these games, you can inquire about how your child could stop when they were required to or could follow directions. Use what they've mentioned to illustrate the ways they can use this in their everyday routines.

Lights: Red Light, Yellow Light, Green Light.

It is a basic activity that you can play indoors or out in the outdoors. It is possible to place yourself at the opposite side of the room, or in a different room with your kid. When you call green light your child is able to move forward in order to "tag your" when you mention yellow light your child should slow down and, when you call red light, your child needs to stop. Your child can't move until you have said green light.

Simon Says

Simon Says is a well-known children's game in which one player can play Simon with the opposite player. The other player must follow the instructions of "Simon Says" each direct must begin by saying "Simon Says" (Simon says"touch your nose", Simon says to hop to one side, Simon says stop hopping on one foot). If the instruction does not begin with Simon says that, then the child must not perform the task as instructed and if they do, then the game ends and you are able to begin again.

Freeze Music

It's a great way to keep your child moving as well as help in controlling their impulses. You can play music that your child can dance to. When the music stops, your child has to stop in the place they're in. Once the music resumes, your child is able to dance.

Mindfulness

Mindfulness can help your family members be into tune to their body, concentrate on their breathing, or become more conscious of their surroundings. There are many ways to integrate mindfulness into your everyday life. Strategies to keep your mind focused throughout your day:

It is possible to teach mindfulness while you take an outing. While you and your child walk, inquire about how feels physical (like the breeze blowing across their face) as well as hear, feel and smell. Ask them to describe how each of these feelings make them feel.

* You can be mindful while eating meals with your child. You can ask the child how food tastes and how that food is beneficial to their body remain strong and healthy.

* You can assist your child to become more aware of their thoughts by asking them to describe what's happening in their minds. Ask them what their thoughts make them feel. If they're thinking of something

negative Ask them how they can change the way they're thinking to feel better.

Journaling

We talked about the idea of starting a gratitude journal, but writing down thoughts and the events of today out of the child's mind is a great general exercise to master. Journaling helps your child work through tough issues, assist them recognize their successes from their day and aid them in tracking the progress they've made. It isn't necessary to have an organized journal to serve a particular purpose. It's enough to have your child record their day, what interests them or might be troublesome to them. They could also simply record whatever thoughts are going through their heads for a certain duration of time. If your child is struggling to be able to commit to the habit of writing, you could keep some prompts in hand to help them write about.

Journal prompts:

* Who is the person that you admire?

• What do you like doing with your favorite friend if you were aware that you were going to be told no?

* What is the best place you'd like to visit?

* What was your most memorable aspect of your weekend?

1. What's your top class in your school?

* What's a thing you'd like to be taught more about at school?

Tell us about your most-loved food?

* Would you rather participate in the sport you love rather than play an instrument? Why?

Which is your most-loved season? Why?

Which is your preferred color? What does it do to you feel?

* What's one thing of kindness that you performed for someone else?

* What's something you'd like to master do?

* Who is your most loved cartoon character? If you had the chance to spend a

whole day with this character , what will you choose to do?

Chapter 7: Working Through Fear, Worry

And Anxiety

The overwhelming fear can be one of the most debilitating emotions. When we're sucked into fear, it's hard to concentrate on anything else as your nervous system will be at alert and our bodies prepare to take the possibility of action. We'll look at the various manifestations of fear as well as the tools needed to deal with them.

Kendra began to sigh time and felt the beginning of tension headache. The entire morning, she was worried about her mom's surgery , and was thinking of calling her phone a second time to check if her father had called with any information. Was it possible that the test showed that her mother was suffering from cancer? Then she was shocked the next second when the phone rang. She was struggling to answer it when she called, "Dad?" She was able to hear the beginning of a pre-recorded credit card solicitation and made an angry sound when she ended the call. She could feel her head start to beat.

As Kendra like us, we all have a fearful feeling at certain points. It is possible that we are prone to worrying regarding things that will never occur, or perhaps we have panic attacks while speaking in front of a crowd. Consider an CBT comprehension of such events.

A QUOTE ABOUT TERMINOLOGY

Psychologists typically distinguish between the following words:

*Fear is triggered in the face of the thing that it is that scares the individual.

However, anxiety involves the perception of a threat that could be real or not.

*Worry is a particular type of anxiety that causes us to constantly think of feared results in situations that involve uncertainty.

For instance, we could suggest that Peter was concerned that he could meet a dog while the route to work. He was anxious when the dog was seen across the road, and felt an intense fear when a huge dog rushed towards him in the park.

The usage we make of these terms is not as precise and I'll be more affixed to the more common usage of these terms.

What's the definition of anxiety?

While excessive anxiety can be harmful, having too less anxiety is not a good thing also. There is an amount of anxiety to inspire us to focus on things that are important to us.

Peter was lying on his the bed, debating whether to press snooze for once more. He checked the time: 6:09 a.m. His train would leave within an hour. Peter thought about the implications of taking an earlier train and being late for his first day's meeting. His boss certainly wouldn't be happy about that. Peter thought about it, switched off his alarm and took himself out of bed.

Peter was experiencing the appropriate level of anxiety, enough to motivate him to get up and out of bed in time, but not too that he was overwhelmed or that it impacted his performance. Similar to Peter We also are able to envision the outcomes of the future that will be influenced by our actions. Be it an initial date, school or an event that is competitive, or something else that we are aware of, our actions impact the outcome. This information can create a mood and a desire to be at our best. Keep in mind that CBT examines the relationships between thoughts, feelings and actions. In the case of anxiety, the thoughts are focused on danger and the emotions include anxiety and anxiety and the behavior includes efforts to avoid the fearful results.

Kendra's anxiety-ridden experiences in waiting for information from her mother appeared like this:

Kendra's anxieties regarding her mother's health cause tension and anxiety, that in turn trigger to have more anxious thoughts. The way she feels and behaves connect and reinforce each other and create a tight-wound anxiety-stricken state.

Although Kendra's anxiety manifested itself as anxiety-inducing worries there are many ways anxiety can manifest itself within our everyday lives.

THE OPTIMAL NUMBER of ANXIETY

In the past 100 years researchers from the animal kingdom Robert Yerkes and John Dodson demonstrated clearly the connection between motivation and emotion. They assessed how fast mice could master a task in the laboratory. In the event of a wrong answer, they received the mice being shocked with varying degrees of degree. The study revealed that low levels of shock lead to slow learning since the mice appeared to be less driven by small punishments. The most extreme levels of shock, however, resulted in slower learning, since the mice appeared to be in a state of arousal which hindered learning.

Psychologists refer to this pattern as one of the "inverted U" due to its shape when graphed.

Humans have the exact similar U-shaped inversion because of their anxiety. Too little or too much can affect our performance, while moderate quantities can boost our performance. For instance moderate doses of stimulants, such as coffee, can boost our energy levels and focus, whereas larger quantities can make us feel anxious and overwhelmed.

There are Many Faces of Fear

Anxiety disorders are among the commonly used psychiatric diagnoses and cover various ailments. In their most recent update which was published in the year 2000, the creators for the Diagnostic and Statistical Manual of Mental Disorders Fifth edition (DSM-5) eliminated OCD as well as PTSD from the category of anxiety conditions, placing every within its own distinct category. There are a variety of reasons behind the changes, however it's widely acknowledged that both conditions have a high level of anxiety. Both PTSD and OCD are also susceptible to the same treatments as does the other anxiety disorder.

SPECIFIC PHOBIA

A fear that is excessively triggered by certain objects could be a sign of an individual fear. One may discover that the fears are exaggerated and it's not much easier to conquer them. Avoidance of the thing or circumstance is frequent.

Every thing can be an object of fear, however, certain types are the most common. These comprise:

* Certain circumstances (e.g. being in an elevator or flying in an airplane)

*Natural environment (e.g. thunderstorms and the heights)

*Animals (e.g., spiders, snakes)

*Blood-injection-injury (e.g., giving blood, getting a shot)

SOCIAL ANXIETY DISTORTION

It's normal for us to experience some anxiety when in social settings in particular when we're conducting or being evaluated. Social anxiety could be a sign of a disorder if it's so severe that it causes extreme stress or causes a person to avoid situations that could create anxiety. The most common fears are:

*Giving a speech or a presentation

* Talking with the group

*Eating in front of other people

*Going to a celebration

Being the focal point

Disagreement with an individual

*Relating with new people

In each of these scenarios there is a fear of appearing embarrassing or having others consider them to be a negative person. One of the reasons that social anxiety last is the difficulty of confirm the fears. What can we do to ensure for instance, that the guests didn't dislike our wedding speech even if they did the expected social thing and claim that it was wonderful? The uncertainty of social situations can exacerbate our anxiety.

PANIC DIORDER

An attack of panic is brief period of intense anxiety typically accompanied by physical signs such as sweating, heart pounding and a shortness of breath. It is often accompanied by changes in our perception of reality, for example experiencing the feeling that things aren't as true (decreolization) and feeling disconnected from our experiences (depersonalization).

The majority of people experience at some point in their lives. It is an illness when it leads to the fear that something catastrophic is taking place (e.g., "I'm having an attack") or the person is in anxiety about the next attack.

The effects of panic attacks can be so severe that those suffering from panic disorder tend to avoid situations where they are likely to be in a panic situation, particularly in situations where it's hard to leave. Some common situations that people avoid include bridges, theaters (especially those that are at the end of an aisle) as well as trains. The avoidance of trains could be a cause for the diagnosis of agoraphobia.

"Part that is human beings' nature includes balancing an equilibrium between anticipating what is to come while accepting the uncertainty of it. The moment you feel anxious, it's a sign the balance is disturbed." Susan M. Orsillo and Lizabeth Roemer The Mindful Approach to Anxiety

GENERALIZED ANXIETY DIORDER (GAD)

Although panic disorder is a fear of imminent risk, GAD involves a more broad anxiety regarding future events. The fundamental issue with GAD is a constant worry about a variety of subjects (as "generalized" implies). One person I know compared GAD to stress from the final exam week, but applied to every circumstance that one encounters. An excessive and uncontrollable anxiety that is a hallmark of GAD results in symptoms such as difficulties in concentrating, insomnia muscles tension and anxiety.

POSTTRAUMATIC STRESS (PTSD) (PTSD)

Anxiety is a natural reaction following an extremely traumatic experience. Anything that is a threat to our physical wellbeing could cause PTSD, such as natural catastrophes, car accidents sexual assaults, muggings and fighting, among others. Watching something horrible occur to someone else, or hearing about a trauma that a loved one has experienced could also make us vulnerable to PTSD.

Following a devastating trauma many people experience symptoms that include:

1. Reimagining and re-living. This can include disturbing memories, nightmares and powerful emotional reactions when being reminded of the experience.

2. Avoidance. This involves avoiding to think about the experience and staying away from people, places, and other things that can trigger a person's memory of what took place.

3. The way we think and feel can change. For instance, we might begin to view the world as an extremely hazardous place, and we may feel in a position of being unable to deal with it. It is also possible that we struggle to trust other people and, in turn, take risks in our daily lives. Also, we are less likely to experience positive emotions , but much more likely to feel negative emotions.

4. Hyper arousal. Our nervous systems are at high alert. It is possible that we have difficulty getting to sleep or concentrating and are constantly monitoring our surroundings to identify danger.

These kinds of reactions are common for almost everyone who has experienced the trauma. To satisfy PTSD requirements, patients have to meet the somewhat arbitrarily set requirement of not lasting for longer than one month.

OBSESSIVE-COMPULSIVE DIORDER (OCD)

The brain is wired in a way to recognize the dangers and to try to stay clear of it. A malfunction in this crucial function can result in OCD. The triggers for OCD are thoughts that are repeated about the negative things that could occur, such as becoming sick, being offended by God or causing fire, or injuring someone else. Naturally, people want to avoid these results, leading to the insatiable desire to eliminate the fear of being obsessive through the compulsions.

Examples of the obsession-compulsion cycle are:

* Fear of becoming sick - Clean hands

* Fear of being hit by an innocent pedestrian. Check the rearview mirror

* Fear of being accused of blasphemy Make a prayer in a ritualized manner

The compulsions can be powerfully reinforced through the negative reinforcement described in. In the same way those with OCD typically feel anxious following the compulsion because they don't have a way to guarantee that what they fear will not occur. In the end, the person suffering from OCD will likely to repeat the compulsion , and could spend a long time trapped in the cycle of obsession and compulsion.

Although many ailments can be improved through various forms therapy, OCD requires a specific treatment. The most successful therapy has been identified as"exposure and reaction prevention which is a form of CBT. It is, as the name implies it involves exposure to fears associated with OCD and the release of the obsessions that cause the condition.

OTHER MODIFICATIONS

Even if you don't fit the the criteria for one or these DSM-5 anxiety disorders, the fear of being anxious can have a negative impact on your life. For instance the subtle and consistent methods we use to make decisions based on fear could affect our lives. Additionally, the manifestations of fear are so widespread that we do not acknowledge the signs. These are the anxieties which keep us trapped in a debilitating condition, but in a life we've never lived.

These kinds of fearful behaviors in:

*Holding ourselves back because of the fear of failure

Avoiding taking reasonable risks because of the fear of the possibility of failure

Living our lives as we should and what others want us to do, is not the way we'd like to live our lives

Averting the vulnerability that comes from real intimacy

Anger that comes from anxiety (e.g. angry at a loved one who is not arriving on time because we were worried about their security)

Consider how fear can manifest in your life. Although fear is intended to protect us but it also hinders us from living our lives fully when we allow it to influence our choices.

Let's look at the tools that can ease anxiety.

Anxiety and your Brain

Imagine that you're taking a relaxing stroll through the woods, and you come across a slimy object in the dirt. The light that is reflected off of the object will reach your eyes and land on the retinas. This causes signals that travel through your neurons' relaying station (the the thalamus) and then into the main visual regions behind the brain. The information then gets transferred to different areas of the brain, including memory regions that associate the object with the idea of "snake."

The idea that you're looking at snakes is transmitted to different areas such as the amygdala located deep within the brain. It is the primary source of experiencing fear and expression of other emotions. What is the brain's way of knowing to be scared of a snake close to your feet on the ground, but not the one that's behind the glass in the Zoo? The amygdala also receives information via the hippocampus. It is essential for understanding the contextual. With the help of your hippocampus, you might even begin to fear when you next walk through the forest, even if do not encounter the snake.

The signals from the amygdala trigger a brain region called the hypothalamus. This will trigger the fight-or-flight reaction of your sympathetic nerve system by releasing stress hormones such as Epinephrine (adrenaline). The hypothalamus also triggers your pituitary glands to secrete hormones in the bloodstream that then go to the adrenal glands (which sit above your kidneys) which causes them to release stress hormones such as cortisol. The survival of humanity is dependent upon this coordinated reaction which allows us to detect and respond to threats such as avoiding the snake.

As it is essential to survive to be afraid of certain stimuli but it's also important to be able to discern when the risk is low to ensure that we're not too fearful. The new knowledge is based on our brains being fed new information. This is something that anxiety-driven avoidance could hinder. For instance, if I always avoid dogs due to the big dog threw me to the ground when I was a young child I'll never understand that this will not be the norm with dogs. When we use mindfulness and cognitive behavior techniques to manage anxiety and fear We are training these brain regions to modify their reactions to situations that make us nervous.

Strategies to deal with Fear, Worry and Anxiety

There are numerous tools to assist you in controlling fear, anxiety, panic and anxiety. These include cognitive, mindfulness, and behavioral techniques.

THINK (COGNITIVE)

When our fear triggers and we're likely to be triggered by thoughts that make us fear more. For instance, if in a state of fear while when we board a plane and we are convinced that the plane is about be crashing, and this intensifies our fear and repeats this cycle (refer on our CBT theory of anxiety for more). When we challenge our anxiety-inducing thoughts and allowing us to break the feedback loop.

A word of caution When we're overwhelmed by anxiety, it can be difficult or impossible to calm ourselves into a state of calm by relying on reason alone. These techniques are likely to be most effective once anxiety takes over, and in conjunction with mindfulness and behavior techniques.

Be aware that anxiety isn't danger-free. Many of us are prone to worry about anxiety in general, believing that it's unsafe to be worried. As uncomfortable as it may be, anxiety isn't detrimental. In addition, being anxious can cause greater anxiety. Remember even during an extreme case of anxiety that your physical, mental and emotional signs will not harm you.

Review the danger's likelihood. The fear of ours can make us believe that what we're scared of will actually happen. However, keep in mind that anxiety disorders have unrealistic expectations given the risk involved, therefore the chance that they'll occur is very low. If you believe that your fears are telling you that something bad could happen then you can use your Core Belief form to test the truth of your assumption. What evidence is for this belief? Does there exist any evidence in support of the idea? Did it happen previously, and if yes how often? If you spot any flaws in your thought process, consider reevaluating the probability that the scenario you are imagining could actually occur with the help of evidence.

Review the seriousness of the threat. Sometimes the mistake that we commit isn't so much about the likelihood of to be a negative outcome, but how serious it could be. For instance, Joe thought it would be awful if people realized that he was stressed out when he was delivering a speech. While he thought about this and realized that others could indeed be aware that he's nervous from the quaver of his voice or the shaking of his hands, but he realized that it's probably not any big deal. He'd already heard speakers who looked nervous prior to and their nervousness did not affect his overall impression of the individual and the caliber of their speech.

Why should we worry? It is difficult to kick, particularly since we believe that we need to be worried. We may think that worrying is a good thing.

*Helps us come up with ways to solve a problem.

*Prevents us from getting blindsided by bad news

*Shows that we care

*Can help things go quite well

*Helps us stay motivated

These notions are usually false. For instance, we cannot escape pain by creating the worst-case scenario. It is just as traumatic in the event that it happened. We also suffer from unnecessary stress due to countless concerns that never come to fruition. If we can see the futility of anxiety and worry, we're more likely shift our focus.

Chapter 8: What Is Cognitive Behavioral

Therapy?

Cognitive Behavioral Therapy was developed in the 1960s by Aaron T. Beck (History of Cognitive Behavior Therapy, n.d.). His research focused on the treatment of patients suffering from depression. He discovered similarities in the thoughts patterns these patents. He was not the only one to notice patterns in their thinking, however, he also observed that when the negative thoughts were assessed by the patient and they were able to change their thoughts to be more focused on the truth and realities of the situation. They were able fight the negative thoughts and made them feel more at ease and content with themselves, their surroundings, people around them, and how they perceived the world.

What is Cognitive Behavioral Therapy?

Cognitive Behavioral Therapy is a kind of psychotherapy that focuses on the way we think, feel and act. These three elements determine our character and the relationships we share and the way in which we live our lives. Cognitive Behavioral Therapy is a method to assist individuals to control their lives and be according to what is the most to them. It's been proven to be a successful treatment for various psychiatric, physical, psychological, and health-related conditions.

Patients with a medical condition will benefit greatly from this type of therapy. The methods, practices and techniques used during sessions can everyone suffering with negative feelings, actions and emotional states. Adults, teenagers and even children can benefit from Cognitive Behavioral tools to deal with the debilitating effects of anxiety, depression or other major emotions that they're struggling to understand. Teens can especially learn useful skills that they will take with them throughout their lives. This could help in their achievement in their school, home and with their relationships.

Cognitive Behavioral Therapy is focused on focusing on staying in the present setting goals, as well as be aware of how thought processes influences behavior. Although it's a short-term treatment, it will provide long-lasting positive outcomes. Through this form of treatment you are able how to change your thinking patterns. Additionally, you will learn how to make connections between your thoughts, emotions and behavior.

Cognitive Behavioral Therapy integrates various techniques in order that patients are able to reach their goals. Each session will include a review of any progress or concerns. The patient is then provided with homework to assist them in moving forward to overcome negative or problematic thinking. Cognitive Behavioral Therapy is used in different methods, each of which focuses on negative thoughts, behavior and feelings that hinder your progress.

Different types of CBT

* Acceptance and Commitment Therapy (ACT)

Acceptance and commitment Therapy incorporates traditional behavior therapy and cognitive Behavior Therapy in an action-oriented method to address mental and behavioral issues. The approach involves people becoming more accepting of their emotions and thoughts instead of absconding with them. It is designed in order for the patient to start making the needed changes and understand how to change their behavior to lead happier lives. This kind of cognitive Behavior Therapy is an effective method for people to confront their fears, manage anxiety and stress and face their fears. The emphasis is on how you communicate with yourself and perceive the world around you because of a negative experience or incident. You start to understand the reasons behind your limitations and the reasons the reasons it keeps holding the door open, as well as you are taught strategies for overcoming and persevering.

* Dialectical Behavior Therapy (BDT)

This kind of Cognitive Behavioral Therapy is often employed to aid people with extreme mood disorders or personality issues. People who struggle to form healthy relationships or who have difficulty with social situations can get benefitted of Dialectical behavior therapy. The primary goal on this treatment is to provide help to the person. It helps you focus on your own strengths and strengths to boost confidence in yourself. It is discussed the limitations of your ideas, thoughts and beliefs that go through your head when you are faced with different situations. Specific goals are established to help you understand the big emotions that are difficult to manage appropriately. Learn to alter how you respond to these emotions , and also how to change your negative thinking ways of dealing with these emotions , so that you can are able to control these emotions. DBT frequently combines mindfulness exercises with effective techniques for recognizing thoughts to help people control their emotions as well as learn how to deal with unpleasant or uncomfortable emotions as well as situations.

* Mindfulness-Based CBT (MBCT)

Mindfulness-Based Cognitive Therapy shows you how to be more conscious to your thought patterns. By increasing your awareness, you'll be in a position to recognize negative thoughts. You can also discover how to change the way you express them and modify them in a way that is more positive and beneficial. This kind of therapy can provide you with a variety of methods and skills that will be beneficial throughout your life.

* Cognitive Processing Therapy (CPT)

Cognitive Processing Therapy (CPT) is typically employed to aid sufferers of severe mental illnesses, such as Post-traumatic Stress Disorder. Through this treatment, people concentrate on the way they deal with traumatic events and how they can alter the actual event. Examine the coping techniques that have been developed to manage the thoughts, behavior and emotions that arise as the event is thought of. You will be able to recognize false thoughts that are running through your mind and to address your negative behaviors as you try to deal with these thoughts whenever they occur. You are taught to analyze situations and discover the truth within them, to help you alter your thought patterns and take control of and conquer the incidents that occurred to you.

You will receive various techniques and exercises that are widely employed in a variety of kinds of Cognitive Behavior Therapy. The most effective ways of finding out the source of your negative beliefs, limiting thoughts, and uneasy feelings are discussed. Additionally, you will learn how you can identify and eliminate the elements that hold you back. Through each of the exercises will give you the fundamentals you require to set goals specific to your needs which will allow you to achieve your goals to the fullest extent possible.

CBT Principles

The principal objective of Cognitive Behavioral Therapy is to teach you how to overcome the mental blockages, behavior and feelings that are holding you behind. As you grow older you'll have to deal with situations that you cannot avoid and have to think about making the right choices. This could result in uncomfortable and overwhelming reactions to the decisions that you make, as you may regret your decision or wish you had the ability to alter your behavior in situations. Cognitive

Behavioral Therapy is effective in helping adolescents overcome their limiting habits and thoughts due to its basic principles.

1. Active Participation

Participants are expected to play an part in the sessions. They assist in defining the goals, formulate actions plans, and then practice strategies that help them move ahead. Being active means being aware of the fact that work will be required to overcome the obstacles that hold them behind. It is also about being willing and open to explore suggested techniques and exercises to help alter how they think and behave. Although some exercises might provide immediate results, and assist them to discern where their thoughts are flawed or areas where behavior should be changed, certain strategies must be used. Staying positive and actively discussing your goals to change will help you achieve huge results.

2. Goal-Oriented

When a person chooses to embark on Cognitive Behavioral Therapy, there are certain issues they wish to tackle and solve.

Identifying the issues will be the initial step in controlling them. It is important to set clear goals and match them with specific treatment strategies that allow them to control and achieve the goals they have set. Your goals should be a reflection of youand you must to be driven to reach them. As we've said before that changing your behavior and thoughts can take time and it is possible that you won't succeed first time around. A clearly defined purpose will ensure that you are engaged to the process.

3. Focus on the Present Moment

Cognitive Behavioral Therapy is uniquely distinct from other forms of therapy as it focuses on the present. The aim is to assist people to recognize their emotions and thoughts and the way they influence their behavior present. The focus isn't often on what happened in the past, unless dealing with these issues will help guide an individual towards their goals. When focusing on what is happening in the present one is able to feel more confident and confident in their ability to control the circumstances they encounter every day, instead of dealing with past events. past.

4. We will provide you with the necessary Tools

Cognitive Behavioral Therapy seeks to show people how to deal with their challenges by using the abilities they already have. CBT can help one develop the skills they already have and think about things from an entirely different perspective, so that they can be able to apply new strategies to situations that were slowing them down. These techniques and skills are invaluable tools that individuals are able to use throughout their lives, to get through the most difficult experiences.

5. Relapse Prevention

People are trained and educated about the most important factors that cause unwanted feelings like depression and anxiety. Through understanding the elements that contribute to the intense mental blockages An individual is able to recognize early warning signs of the signs that could lead to the possibility of return to depression. If these symptoms are identified an individual is able to adjust their behavior and employ the correct techniques that allow them to avoid getting trapped by their feelings or thoughts.

6. Time-Limited

Cognitive Behavioral Therapy is a method to assist individuals to attain their goals within only a few minutes. Certain individuals might be capable of overcoming their barriers in only one or two sessions. These treatment plans that are shorter provide people with greater hope and confidence that they can to overcome the obstacles that have been hindering them.

7. Structured

Cognitive Behavioral Therapy provides individuals with a predetermined sequence of actions to follow that will help them achieve their goal in only a few minutes. If you're seeing therapy sessions, they will typically begin with addressing the problem in question and introducing techniques or tools to tackle the issue and then assigning an homework task for the client to complete prior to their next appointment. When they return in the next session, it will begin with a discussion of the way in which homework assignments went and what adjustments can be made and a new homework task will be assigned. The sessions are easy and structured that's why it a great way to help people better manage their thoughts, emotions and behaviours.

8. Dispels Negative Thinking

The ability to control one's thinking is a major goal in Cognitive Behavioral Therapy. Negative thoughts can be the cause of numerous issues and setbacks people face. Cognitive Behavioral Therapy gives individuals specific strategies to recognize the root of negative thinking, reverse it, and develop positive thoughts that are both empowering and positive. The way to address negative thoughts that the person may or might not know about is the way they'll be able adopt more beneficial methods of thinking.

9. Incorporates Various Techniques

Cognitive Behavioral Therapy utilizes a range of strategies during the sessions and on homework assignments. The participants will be taught a variety of methods they can use to enhance their lives. These include breathing exercises, meditation as well as relaxation training and exposure therapy, in addition to other. These methods (which will be explained in more detail , along with other) are assessed by the individual to ensure they are able to identify the most effective techniques that will prove most beneficial to them.

What can CBT do for you?

The purpose of cognitive behavioural therapy is to assist you in understanding your thinking process and patterns. New patterns are formed by analyzing and analyzing the past as well as identifying triggers and setting goals that help you to control your thoughts and lead happier and more fulfilled life.

When you are a teenager this might seem like a complicated process. At a very early age, we begin to act in line with our thinking. In our current time and age, it's never been more crucial for teenagers to be able to spot and redirect their negative thoughts.

There are many aspects that Cognitive Behavioral Therapy can help you take control of, including:

• How to recognize the negative thoughts in your mind.

* How to manage large emotions.

* How to control anger.

• How to cope with loss or grief.

* Strategies to deal with trauma.

* How to improve your sleep.

• How to manage difficult relationships.

The primary advantage is understanding the way your thoughts influence your mood and behavior. It aims to improve your ability to recognize negative thoughts and to re-programme your thoughts so that you are able to manage anxiety, stress and other difficulties better.

Cognitive Behavioral Therapy can be used to help effectively treat:

* Anxiety

* Focus and attention concerns

* Chronic pain

* Depression

* Eating disorders

* Obsessive-compulsive disorders

* Sleep issues

* Trauma

It's used to tackle the myriad of issues that arise from thoughts and behaviour.

Cognitive Behavioral Therapy can help to break down problems into smaller specific goals. The most intense emotions, such as depression and anxiety are categorized into smaller categories (thoughts behavior, emotions, thoughts). Then, strategies are offered to deal with each of the types. Through breaking down the challenges and problems in this way you'll be able to identify the root of the issue and develop an appropriate strategy to address and manage these issues.

How CBT can help improve Areas of Your Life

Teens must deal with many emotional and stressful situations. A lot of them are quickly dealt with and could lead to poor choices as well as low self-esteem. Teens who participate in Cognitive Behavioral Therapy usually discover a solution for their anxiety about issues like taking tests as well as time management, speaking at school, socializing as well as setting and achieving goals which ensure a positive life after leaving high school. Every aspect of your life can be affected by cognitive behavioural therapy.

Relationships

The way you interact with others has a direct effect on how you perceive your self and others around you. Connecting with other people is vital to social development, however, having deep connections with them can improve the image you project of yourself. The relationships you share with your siblings, parents and friends or with your the person you love dearly. It could also refer to the relationships you have with your teachers and classmates.

In the context of the relationships aspect that you are in, make note of the following important factors.

• Which of your relationships is working good for you?

* What elements of these relationships work well?

* Where are you having trouble with your relationships?

* What is your way of communicating with these people?

* Do you have enough time with those who are in these relationships?

* What's your relationship to these people?

Cognitive Behavioral Therapy will help you understand how you communicate with people around you and help boost your self-confidence and build lasting relationships. It will help you understand the way you perceive others see you , and how other people's behavior and words affect how you view yourself and how you behave. Learn how to create a clear picture of yourself , which will make you feel more at ease and secure around other people.

Make a list of all the people (friends and family members, siblings and other) that you have a connection with. What would you do to improve your relationships with them? Consider what thoughts, feelings or behavior could influence the relations (good as well as bad).

School/Work

A few teens are in or have already entered the workforce while taking classes. Some teens are focusing on extracurricular activities and school. In any case, it is a major part of the lives of teens. Because school is the center of your life for the majority of your time as a young adult it is vital that this part of your life brings you joy. If you are suffering from depression, anxiety, or any other stressors it will make you less content in this part that you live in.

Teens need to be taught how to see the meaning of their schoolwork as well as extracurricular activities and the jobs they will be working during their time. This will help them go on to careers that will give their lives more meaning and joy. Some teenagers are not motivated enough to feel excited about this field Others are insecure or anxious of their abilities (or or, in their minds or in their minds, the lack of) to excel in this particular area.

In assessing this part in your own life take a look at:

* What are your thoughts about being a student with a high-quality education.

* Which classes at the school do you find most enjoyable?

* Are there any classes that you need to spend more time in?

* What other other activities are you involved in?

• Which do you like?

What is the extent to which like your current position?

* What are you contemplating following after graduation?

Spirituality

Spirituality is the reason we feel connected to the world that surrounds us. Some people experience their spirituality through following the religion of their choice, while others discover it through meditation and yoga while others experience this connection when in the natural world. Spirituality provides us with an additional meaning and purpose. It reminds us that we're part of something greater than what we perceive as well as experience through our everyday lives.

If you are thinking about this aspect that you are in, you should ask yourself:

* What is important to you?

* What do you truly are passionate about?

* Are your actions purposeful?

Are you a part of something that is meaningful to you?

* What would you like other people to think of you?

Health

Being healthy and living a balanced life may not be an issue as a teenager. Most teens aren't worried about the way that fast food and chips can affect their health in the future. However, bad food choices and lack of exercise and sleeping in too much can affect our mental as well as our physical health.

Chapter 9: Perfection And Its Effect On

Mental Health

A person's claim that they're a perfectionist makes an excellent impression. But, you're not sure what's behind the words. Perfectionists can lead to mental illness and well-being when it gets out of control. It can have a significant effect on physical and mental health. Perfectionists may suffer from anxiety, suicidal thoughts as well as depression. But, these aren't the only mental health issues one may be confronted with. There are other mental health issues that are experienced by perfectionists, like Obsessive-Compulsive Disorder.

Perfectionists are subject to negative thinking processes which can trigger emotional problems. Being unable to meet the standard can cause the feeling of guilt, lower self-esteem and anxiety-related issues. Some people feel that they are not worthy when they are unable to complete their tasks that meet their expectations and, if the thoughts persist, they may even trigger suicidal behavior.

Furthermore, perfectionists can lead to mental illness because they believe that they aren't worthy of love and acceptance from other people. Although they may be the role models for others they may feel they're not good enough.

Is perfectionistism a sign of low self-esteem?

One of the main reasons why perfectionism can lead to poor mental health is linked to self-esteem. If you feel low self-esteem the defense mechanisms you have developed perfectionism to increase your self-esteem. When you have low self-esteem and you feel insecure within. You'll try to be the most attractive person at a gathering, earn the highest marks, or even be the most productive employee at your work place. If you're striving for perfection, you could become obsessed with perfection as a sign.

As you try to increase your self-esteem, you can set very high standards of yourself. This can lead to unrealistic goals, such as getting 99% marks on your maths test, but considering it as being a failure.

For perfectionists, everything's in black and white. They will not accept anything less than perfection, which is the reason they are often disappointed and angry with themselves. Every little mistake can cause them to feel like they've committed a crime or committed a sin.

Perfectionism can be an indicator of low self-esteem , and in the event of not being handled properly it could lead to mental health issues.

The connection between perfectionism and anxiety

Anxiety and perfection are inextricably linked. In the event of making mistakes, we are afraid the possibility of being criticized for our mistakes or suffer negative consequences. This anxiety can cause stress. A perfectionist tries to avoid making errors and perform to the highest level of excellence. But they are also human and there always exists a possibility of human mistakes. A fear of even the tiniest error in their work can cause anxiety.

Anxiety disorders can cause perfectionists to contribute to their typical. It is because those who are perfectionists are obsessed with getting their task done in a better way. This obsession can cause anxiety and mental health issues. There are two kinds of anxiety disorders associated with perfectionists:

1. Generalized Anxiety Disorder

Have you ever wondered if you are making the right choice? Are you deserving of a reward you've received, increase or promotion? These are a few questions you'll be asked when you suffer from a generalized anxiety disorder. It is characterized by the anxiety of the feeling of not having enough worthiness. This can cause you to experience an uncontrollable fear about certain areas of your existence.

2. Social Anxiety Disorder

If you are a perfectionist and worry about how others might judge you, there is social anxiety. There are times when people feel high levels of anxiety fearing being judged before others. This is because of the fear of not being adequate enough. The perfectionists might experience excessive level of stress and social anxiety that can cause them to feel overwhelmed.

The idealists view things as absolutes. There is a choice between right and wrong, with no gray area or middle ground.

OCD and Perfectionism

It's difficult to deal with perfectionists to deal with, however what happens if you're also obsessive-compulsive? OCD is the abbreviation for Obsessive Compulsive Disorder. Most of the time, people who are perfectionists are prone to developing OCD as an unhealthy form of perfectionism. It is possible to have an obsessive-compulsive disorder if you exhibit these symptoms:

1. Particularly in regards to things that are done in a specific manner

It is important to have some boundaries to help you. If it reaches the boundaries, it becomes an obsession. It is possible to develop OCD in the event that you believe things are carried out in the way you think is the right way to do things. Anything that isn't performed as you intended to see it done would be considered unacceptable by you.

2. You exhibit high-checking behaviors.

There is a possibility that you suffer from OCD signs if you continually have to check on everything or anyone for instance, checking if the doors are locked, whether the stove is off or not, and so on. You might feel dissatisfied when you're not sure about the situation.

In the event of feeling uncertain it is possible that you have the fear of making mistakes. Little things such as opening the stove or leaving your door to your house open could cause you to be nervous, leading to irregular checking pattern.

You or someone you know is suffering from OCD perfectionist, they will be sure to check the same thing over and over. They might feel like they're losing their minds but will not let it go. This could cause you to lose confidence in yourself and cause you to feel even worse.

3. Controlling behavior

If your obsession with perfection has increased and you believe you be in control of everything like your thoughts, you could be suffering from OCD. OCD sufferers OCD is likely to label any thought as bizarre or distressing as uncontrollable because it's not within their control.

How do you deal with OCD?

If you've recognized your obsessional-compulsive behaviors You must attempt to overcome it. If visiting a healthcare doctor isn't your primary choice, then you may take the initiative to tackle the issue yourself. If the situation seems out of control, it is best to seek out medical assistance.

Here are some things you can try:

1. Mindfulness Meditation

Engage in mindful meditation to help you focus on being present in your life This will make you more conscious of your feelings and thoughts. Meditation can help relax us and make us less stressed and distracted about anything, even being flawless.

All you need to do is relax and enjoy taking a seat in a calm area. Concentrate on breathing while closing your eyes. Try this for 15 minutes every day.

2. Cognitive Behavioral Therapy

Another option you can consider is using Cognitive behavioral methods. This can include cognitive restructuring and behavioral tests. These can help you understand that it's okay making mistakes, and admit to flaws.

Furthermore, cognitive therapy assists in the examination of the beliefs we hold about ourselves. Cognitive therapy can also help with the prevention of response and exposure that can assist in coping with the feeling of losing control.

This is a great option when you go through extreme behavior checks or are constantly trying to correct things.

However, the most effective way is to talk with the therapist you trust and listen to their suggestions.

The procrastination-perfectionism paralysis

One of the most significant consequences of perfectionists is the tendency to procrastinate. Perpetually, people who are perfectionists delay their work and are anxious and stressed. They are unable to get started because they're frozen because they anxiety that they won't accomplish the task properly.

They put off the tiniest and most simple thingslike getting rid of items of clothing that are no longer needed, drawers and files and reconciling accounts or organizing their clothing in the closet. These tasks are straightforward and straightforward, but they can be very laborious, and the act of procrastination can make it appear impossible.

The more crucial issues may appear more challenging since they require more commitment, time and a higher risk of failure that is why many people put off doing these tasks.

They often put off updating their resumes, facing situations and working towards their personal goals. It can impact their lives negatively. They make up various excuses like I'm overwhelmed or it's tiring and I'm overwhelmed with work to complete, etc. These excuses turn into convenient excuses that result in failing to make any meaningful adjustments to their lives.

9 Tips to Stop Procrastination

Step 1. Make sure you are focusing only on one thing at a at a time.

Being an perfectionist, lack of focus because of the belief that you can't perform the task correctly is a main reason for procrastinating. This is why, to improve your concentration, focus on one thing at a moment. If you have a larger project or task, break it down into smaller pieces. the task into smaller ones and focus on finishing only one thing at a. Make sure to take five-minute breaks after each task has been completed to ensure you can increase your concentration.

For instance:

If you're an undergraduate student, you will are required to take eight tests for, you must prepare. Concentrate on just one exam at one time. If the vast outline of your course overwhelms you, break it up into smaller parts. The more small goals you set, the more easy it will be to reach these goals. Make short breaks when you reach the point. In this way, you'll be satisfied when you have accomplished something and while doing so you'll feel motivated to try more.

Step 2. Create to-do lists

Create a habit of writing your tasks you need to do in a single day. Make a list of them by prioritizing those that are most important and then the less important tasks. This will allow you to see how much you have to accomplish and from the point you're supposed to start. For many people, many tasks difficult to manage. A list of tasks can help them see what they must do.

For instance:

Write down all the tasks you need to complete today. Prioritize them by putting the most important task to the least important. You can either check off or cancel the items on your list when they are completed , to give yourself a satisfaction of having things accomplished.

Step 3. Create a timetable using the details

Create a schedule for the week , or one day that you have particulars. Write down all the tasks you need to complete and the amount of time you must devote for each one. Make sure to break down the more important tasks and projects into smaller projects and write them down in your schedule, with the appropriate time allocated. This will allow you to finish the task on time and a bigger project may not seem as daunting in the end.

Step 4. Sort

The proper planning and keeping the day organized will reduce procrastination. Be sure you have the tools and materials that you require to complete the task at hand to avoid having to search for things during the course of your work. If we don't have everything planned out, no is organized, and we don't know what to do with each task or job, and also what else to do it becomes easy to put off completing the task.

For instance:

There is a deadline you must be able to meet. One deadline can cause you to feel overwhelmed make sure to break your project down into smaller pieces. When you begin to complete the smaller tasks you'll feel more confident in completing the whole task.

Second, arrange your tasks according to your preferred method. The most challenging tasks should be reserved to the time during the day that you are most effective. For some, it could be in the morning, while for others they could be at the night. This can help you complete them faster.

Step 5. Start and take Action

Procrastination linked to perfection makes you afraid of every single thing. It is possible that you are afraid of starting something new, and you'll put off taking it on. However difficult it might seem, you must begin your project or task and complete it. When you start working on it the task, it will become simpler to complete.

For instance:

If you're assigned an assignment, don't begin working on it at the very end of the day. Get started as soon as you can. This will get you closer to completing the task. Once you've started, opt for the best approach and adhere to a set timeframe.

Step #6. Utilize the Eisenhower Matrix

The Eisenhower matrix is an easy method to stop procrastination. It is necessary to make four boxes and classify them according to urgency and significant tasks important, not urgent but important crucial but not urgent but not essential, and neither urgent nor crucial.

First box is likely to include urgent and crucial tasks written in the boxes. The tasks you'll need to complete in a matter of minutes. The third box, which contains important , but not crucial tasks, is put off until later. In the meantime the third box would contain things that are urgent but not crucial. They could be assigned to someone else because you may have too many things to do. The fourth, but not the least box is likely to have none of the urgent or vital tasks. The tasks can be removed to lessen the burden placed on your shoulders.

The Eisenhower matrix can help you prioritize your tasks more quickly. Many times we tend to put off or delay on tasks they consider difficult or difficult to accomplish. By labeling them, you will be aware of the urgency and make you take action accordingly.

Step 7. Self-motivation

People who are perfect often lack motivation to accomplish the work they must complete. In addition, increasing your motivation levels will result in a decrease in procrastination. It is possible to improve your motivation in many ways.

For instance:

It is possible to read motivational books or quotes and remind you that it's okay to make mistakes and set standards for yourself. For some, looking at their reflection and reminding themselves that they don't need to be perfect, but they can try to be the best they can is a great way to increase the motivation level and for some engaging with people who inspire them is another option. The goal is to boost self-motivation and end procrastination. Motivation for every person can be attributed to a variety of things. Therefore, determine what drives you, and then stop putting off the task.

Step 8. Pause and enjoy some fresh air

If you're feeling anxious and stressed or when the deadline is approaching and you are unable to focus on your task take an exercise or take a brief break in the fresh air. After you've felt better, you can think about what you have to accomplish and determine how you will complete the task or project in time for the time frame. You can then go back to your work.

Fresh air can be a boon in times of stress. If you live near a park you can take a stroll or lie on the grass for a short time. This will help relieve tension and allow you to focus on finishing your work in time.

Step 9. The practice of meditation and exercise will to improve your focus and reduce stress. It is a good idea to set some time each morning to sit and sit and meditate. Simple mindfulness exercises can help you focus and improve efficiency during the course of your day.

Exercise and morning walks are also extremely helpful in putting an end to procrastination. Exercise boosts your levels of energy and helps clear your mind and improves your self-confidence. It will help you be more efficient and effective throughout the day and go a long way towards ending the procrastination-perfectionism cycle.

A Few Healthy Alternatives to Perfection

The pressure of perfection is exhausting and draining physically and mentally. It causes you to think that you'll never be enough and you doubt your own worth. It is impossible to be kind to oneself or accept other peoples praise if they believe they're not enough.

The perfectionist may feel angry or angry when they commit mistakes or fail to do something that is up to their expectations.

Furthermore, perfectionists have trouble when it comes to delegating work since they're unable to believe in others.

However, those who are perfectionists can gain relief from their problems by looking at and implementing the options below.

1. Excellence

Instead of using perfectionists as a standard, strive for excellence. The word "excellence" leaves room for imperfections, whereas flawless doesn't. Furthermore, when you use excellence as a norm it leaves the possibility of improvement and growth that will result in you not being too difficult on yourself when you tell yourself that there's always more to discover and learn about the world around you and people in your life.

Making a mistake and apologizing the responsibility can help you learn from it and avoid the need to repeat the same error. This kind of approach is more healthy because it doesn't cause obsession like perfectionist can.

With a focus on excellence, we give ourselves compassion and understanding not only for ourselves , but also for other people. This lets us treat others with kindness and compassion even when they don't behave in the manner we prefer to or when we make mistakes.

2. It's the Good Enough Approach

The other option is the "good enough" method. While we've discussed it before, this is an option that we should be aware of. If you aren't able to accomplish something or perform something does not meet your expectations choose the best-of-the-best method. It's what you are able to do the best.

We need healthier alternatives to perfectionism?

Perfectionists typically choose to pursue one of the different mindsets discussed in the previous paragraphs when they realize and get it made clear by a professional that their desire for perfection has surpassed healthy boundaries.

PerfECTIONISM can cause mental health problems like depression and anxiety and may lead to suicidal thoughts and suicides.

PERFECTIONISM IS THE GAP BETWEEN EXPECTATIONS AND REALITY, SO THERE MAY BE THE DANGER THAT SUCH INDIVIDUALS MIGHT HURT THEMSELVES OR TAKE THEIR OWN LIVES WHEN THEY CANNOT HANDLE THE OVERWHELMING STRESS AND UNHAPPINESS IN THEIR LIVES.

Therefore, once PERFECTION IS not anymore a source of benefit for us in OUR everyday lives and at work it is imperative that we examine OURSELVES to figure OUT the reasons why this is so and SEEK Assistance to make the necessary changes in OUR mindsets and the way we live OUR lives.

Overcoming Perfectionism

When you've finished this book I'd like you to feel incredibly empowered and believe that you have the power to make a change in your life, or to remain a perfectionist. But, I think you wouldn't have read until the very end of the book if PERFECTIONIST was working for you.

Before we dive into the solutions, I WANTED to say something important about the path that we all undertake in life. There isn't a single ideal way to go for anyone of US. Every path will have some worth, though some will be more valuable than OTHERS. The most dangerous thing we can do is to do nothing. Doing nothing is often what Perfectionists do since it's a challenge to find a perfect path forward. ALL ANY OF US CAN DO IS CHOOSE A ROUTE AND MOVE OUT FORWARD WITH FLEXIBILITY AND PERSEVERANCE.

10 Action Steps to Follow

The good thing is that you are able to deal the pressure of being a perfectionist by taking a few steps. They are:

Step 1: Acknowledge the receipt

There is no way to resolve an issue if they do not admit that there's an issue at all. Don't forget that perfectionists aren't an all-bad thing but if you're an idealist and it's creating problems within your professional or personal life, it's the right time to acknowledge the cause of problems and begin working to correct the issue.

Step 2: Accept the fact that you're permitted to make mistakes

You're human and, like all of us is likely to fail because it is part of human nature. Don't establish standards for yourself or others that you can't meet. You may try to improve things, but don't think that they will be perfect since this is the way life works. Be over the fear of being embarrassed and being snubbed by the society when you make mistakes. Everyone has faults, and that's okay since this is the way we are.

Step 3 Step #3: Know the necessary standards to deal with the situation

Learn the appropriate standards to be met in every situation. If you're not sure what you should know, ask for clarification because assumptions are generally untrue and waste time. Your boss might have requested details on a particular issue to provide background information. If you believe he'll need it to present then you could waste your time in creating a polished presentation to present to an employee.

Step #4: Consider worst-case scenarios

Many of us believe in perfection as a means of to avoid failure, but this usually leads to the opposite of action. Instead, when confronted with a challenge take a look at the worst-case scenario, and consider how likely it is that it will happen since you have the power to take action to prevent it from happening.

Another way to do this is to create a list of possible scenarios as well as probable outcomes, discussing it with someone you be confident in to help you navigate the situation and get rid from any thoughts that are negative.

Step 5 Step 5: Retract your attention away from "black or white" or "all or all or nothing" thoughts.

Remember that life isn't simple and there are many ways to think and accomplish things. Don't let one mistake determine who you are And remember that everyone has mistakes.

Step #6: Take the "good enough" approach

This method is a compromise between not completing your task and being obsessed with being perfect as you haven't done anything whatsoever. This does not mean that you can take it to justify poor work. This means that you are able to complete your work and not be sucked to inaction due to the pressure to finish the job flawlessly.

Step #7 Change your internal dialogue

Your inner dialogue is affected through your unconscious mind. It exposes your thoughts, beliefs and opinions. As you begin to move away from the perfectionist path begin to notice your internal dialog and replace the talk of perfection and self-reflections that are negative with positive options.

Step 8: Don't be intimidated by the expectations set by people around you

Do not be pulled or pushed according to their norms. Do what you feel is right because this is what's right. Limit the influence of others' influence on your life by taking control of your own life. Your confidence in yourself will increase while other people's opinions are less important. Soon, you will notice that you are more confident.

Step 9: Set yourself time-limits

Time constraints will guarantee that you don't work on something until it's finished. Deadlines are ideal to use for this. Use the help of a timer, so that you must end your work after the timer has gone off.

Step #10: Practice

Do what you can do to overcome the mindset of perfection. Keep the 6th step in mind and work on being "good enough" rather than being perfect.

Chapter 10: Overcoming Perfectionism

A variety of methods can be employed to overcome perfectionist tendencies and live your the life you want to live. It's possible to think there's no way to overcome perfection and stop it from reappearing throughout your life. The good news is that these easy and tried-and-true strategies can help you get to your goals. It's all you have to do is allow your mind to work in a different way. Be positive about everything and reminding yourself that you're human will transform your way of living your life. Your behavior will change eventually and your values will gradually become more rational thoughts.

Determine the pros and cons of aiming for perfection.

Every decision and every inclination is accompanied by pros and pros and. It is important to understand the ways that perfection can positively or harm you. It's a benefit in some instances, but it's often a source of trouble majority of the time. What are the motivations you have observed in the past that have led you to adopt a perfectionist perspective on your life? Do your present actions stem by pure motives or are you simply seeking applause or praise? Since you began using perfectionist principles in your life, have you noticed a difference or did it not? It's your choice to decide how you'll handle this particular process however, it's best to be honest with yourself. You could have a loved ones to support you to give you an impartial view about your conduct.

Love yourself regardless of your imperfections.

You were brought to this world as a flawed human. You cried and peed whenever you desired to. As you got older you saw how flawed you could be. Everyone is flawed however, unlike a lot of people, you're probably not happy with yourself because of it. You're emotionally wounded and feel like you're beating yourself up each day because of the person you aren't. You're so self-critical on yourself you're constantly unsatisfied with the person you've never be. You're imperfect. It's the truth. There are no perfect people however love can be shared.

It is possible to still feel love and be shared. You must learn to accept yourself in spite of the flaws you have because they are a reason that you are unique.

Being a mother myself I have found it simple to establish the standard high regarding the way I'd like to raise my children. It is always a matter of ideals about the food I'm supposed to provide my kid, the amount of television she should watch and how she should be controlled. This is a amazing article that praises mothers for what they're doing, regardless of whether it's right or incorrect. Every mother is doing the best they can, even if it's different from what an other mother would do. At the end of the day I am reminded of how to appreciate my efforts that I am doing regardless of the fact that other mothers might disagree.

Here's the post I discovered in Facebook with the title Beautifully BellaFaith that I found to be encouraging:

"To the mom who's nursing Congratulations! It's a wonderful present for your child, in whatever length of time you can handle! You're a great mommy.

For the mother who is formula-feeding: Doesn't it incredible? It's amazing to think of the time that a child with a mother who could not produce enough food would suffer But today? Better living with the chemistry! You're a great mom.

For the moms who cloth diaper These fluffy bums are most adorable, and they're so nice to the bank account. You're a wonderful mom.

To the mom who uses disposable diapers The diapers can hold a lot and it's great not to worry about leakage or laundry! You're a great mom.

To the mom that is home with her children I can only imagine that it's not easy doing your job however, to get to spend the time you have with your children is surely an amazing experience. You're a wonderful mom.

To the moms who work to support her family: It's great that you're able to stay true to your job as a positive influencer for your kids in numerous ways. It's wonderful. You're a great mother.

To the mom who was forced to feed her kids at the drive-through all week long because you're just too exhausted to cook or grocery shop You're feeding your children and I'm sure they're not complaining! Sometimes, sanity can be located in a red container with a large white M. You're a wonderful mother.

The mom who provided her children a breakfast cooked at home for lunch and dinner during the past week: Fantastic! A healthy diet is crucial and the kids are learning to appreciate healthy food choices from an early age. This is a great benefit to them for the rest of their lives. You're a wonderful mom.

For the mom with children who are sitting in a quiet place and maintaining their manners in the restaurant with all the glamour: Kudos, it takes an enormous amount of discipline to keep the order of children in a space that they aren't allowed to run around. You're a great mom.

Conclusion

The majority of us were raised to believe the idea that being an absolute perfectionist can be beneficial. It's not a bad thing to be a perfectionist if it can benefit us, and we experience the results both personally and professionally. However, there will be a point at which being a perfectionist no anymore working for us. We're missing deadlines due to the fact that we aren't getting an assignment completed to our liking or we spend all day at work while ignoring our families and acquaintances. At some point when we are aware that perfectionism can trigger numerous emotional issues, and could affect negatively our lives.

The book sheds some insight into the issue and provided readers with strategies to address the issue. I hope this book will help you lead a healthier and more productive life.